LOU HENRY HOOVER

GALLANT FIRST LADY

LOU HENRY HOOVER

GALLANT FIRST LADY

By

HELEN B. PRYOR, M.D.

ILLUSTRATED WITH PHOTOGRAPHS

AND A MAP

❦

DODD, MEAD & COMPANY

NEW YORK

Copyright © 1969 by Helen B. Pryor

All rights reserved

*No part of this book may be reproduced in any form
without permission in writing from the publisher*

Library of Congress Catalog Card Number: 69–16201

*Printed in the United States of America
by The Cornwall Press, Inc., Cornwall, N. Y.*

DEDICATED TO

The Mid-Peninsula YWCA, housed in the Lou Henry Hoover Memorial Building, 4161 Alma Street, Palo Alto, California, in the belief that it will continue to have a program for women and girls which reflects Mrs. Hoover's ideals.

PREFACE

Lou Henry Hoover was chosen as the subject of this biography in the hope that some of the present generation may come to know a courageous First Lady of the United States, and may gain something of her strength, ability, and common sense as reflected in her story.

Married to an extraordinary man, she kept his interests always uppermost, although she had many worth-while projects of her own. She remained close by him in difficult and dangerous situations, and as an intellectual partner she supported him in attaining his objectives.

In her primary role of wife, mother, and homemaker, she was thoroughly at ease under all sorts of conditions, and her sympathetic interest in the welfare of others encompassed people of the whole world. Throughout her life she demonstrated her belief in the worth and dignity of the individual. Her interest in all races of people and her outgoing friendliness were natural developments of this belief.

A thread of history is carried through each chapter of her biography because so many historical events shaped the pattern of Lou Henry Hoover's life.

My gratitude goes to all who have contributed material for the biography: the late Honorable Herbert Hoover for permission to quote a few paragraphs from his *Memoirs;* Mrs. Delano Large, niece of Mrs. Hoover, for some old family portraits, letters, and a diary; Mrs. William Vowles, granddaughter, for personal recollections; the late Miss Susan Dyer, schoolmate and close friend; Mrs. Frederic C. Butler, who was secretary to Mrs. Hoover in 1918 and who joined the White House staff in 1930; to Mrs. Allan Campbell who, as Miss Mildred Hall, was personal secretary to Mrs. Hoover from February 8, 1927, to August 18, 1934; and to Mrs. Melissa King Clark, Mrs. Helen Green White, Mrs. Dare Stark McMullin, and Miss Bernice Miller, Hoover secretaries.

In the biography, all direct quotations from Mrs. Hoover's speeches were taken from the files of newspaper clippings in the Lou Henry Hoover Collection.

I appreciate the cooperation of Dr. Glenn Campbell, director of the Hoover Institution on War, Revolution, and Peace, Dr. Rita Campbell, archivist, and Mrs. Eileen Shaw, assistant to the archivist.

Also I am greatly indebted to my husband, Roy Pryor, to Mrs. Frederic Paist, Mrs. Howard Seifert, Mrs. William Boggess, Mrs. Dori White, and to my daughter Mrs. George Bartlett, all of whom read and criticized the manuscript, and to Mrs. George Perry who typed it.

CONTENTS

ILLUSTRATIONS

Following page 112

The pictures used as illustrations in this biography came from the Crandall Collection in the Lou Henry Hoover Archives.

Mrs. Herbert Hoover served as National President of the Girl Scouts.

Phineas and Jenny Weed, grandparents of Lou Henry Hoover.

Mr. and Mrs. Charles D. Henry, the parents of Lou Henry Hoover.

Lou Henry at the age of nine, with her sister Jean, seventeen months, November, 1883.

At ten, Lou Henry was already devoted to outdoor sports.

Snapshots in a family album show the busy, happy Stanford College days of Lou Henry and Herbert Hoover, about 1896: Lou Henry as chief cook, aided by Marian Dale, for a campfire meal; in the chemistry laboratory; and on the archery field.

Young Herbert Hoover shared in many of these activities.

Mrs. Hoover found great delight in the company of her beloved grandchildren, Allan, Junior, and Andy, children of her son, Allan.

The Hoover family group include, left to right, Herbert, Junior; his wife Margaret, with their son Peter; Mrs. Hoover, holding their lively daughter, Peggy Ann; Herbert Hoover, Senior; and his son Allan.

Lou Henry Hoover was ever an enthusiastic and expert horsewoman.

The living room of Rapidan Camp, near Washington, D. C., favorite weekend retreat of the Hoovers and their fortunate guests.

Lou Henry Hoover, gracious and gallant First Lady of the United States.

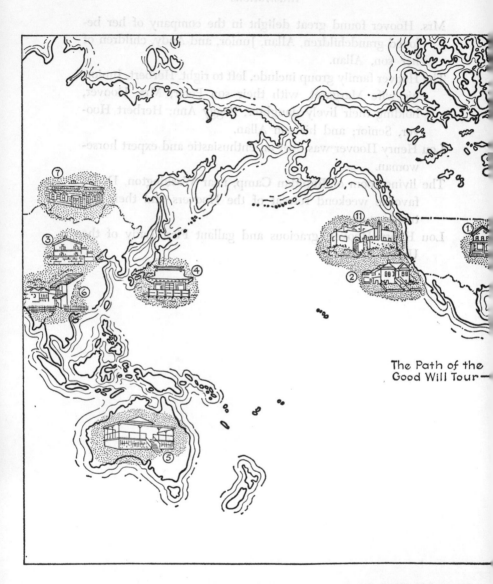

The Path of the
Good Will Tour—

THE VARIED HOMES OF THE HOOVER

1 Waterloo, Iowa
2 Monterey, Calif.
3 Tientsin, China
4 Yokohama, Japan
5 Kalgoorie, Australia
6 Burma

7 Irkutsk, Russia
8 London, England
9 2300 S St. Wash., D.C.
10 The White House
11 Stanford, Calif.
12 Waldorf Astoria Tower

FAMILY THROUGHOUT THE WORLD

I

EARLY LIFE

•

1874–1893

IT WAS A BRIGHT DAY in early spring of the year 1882. In the sewing corner of the dining room of one of the larger houses in Waterloo, Iowa, a little girl turned anxiously to her mother.

"Is my dress all right? May I put it on now?"

Mrs. Henry examined the small plaid garment carefully. "Yes," she replied with a smile, "you have turned a good hem and you may wear the dress to show your father."

With the dress over her arm, Lou ran eagerly upstairs to her room. As she passed the window on the landing, her eye was caught by a red kite snared in the branches just outside. Dropping the dress, she threw open the window. At the foot of the tree stood a small neighbor boy, staring up disconsolately. His face brightened at the sight of her.

"Can you get it loose?" he called.

Lou never hesitated. "I'll try," she answered and leaned out precariously. She stretched as far as she could, but the kite stayed just out of reach. She stretched again, and might have gone tumbling out herself had the wind not blown a branch within her reach. She caught it and pulled until the kite was in her hand.

"There!" she called triumphantly, as she set it free. "There's your kite." For just a moment as she watched her grateful little friend run off with the tugging kite, Lou was tempted to leave the new dress where it lay and slip outdoors to play. It was a glorious day for kite flying, tree climbing, and all the other tomboyish activities she loved. But then she thought of the tiny stitches she had so painstakingly put into that hem. Domesticity won. She caught up the dress and ran into her room.

Her dress changed, Lou slipped on her coat and waited impatiently on the front-porch steps for her father to come home. Today was her eighth birthday and she wanted to show him her new plaid dress. When she saw him coming she ran to meet him.

"Look, Papa, this is my new dress. I helped Mama make it, too."

"What a clever little girl," he said as he gathered her into his arms. Inside the house he turned to kiss his wife and then took his accustomed place in front of the pot-bellied stove with his hands behind his back and his feet apart. Lou, who liked to imitate her father in every way possible, stood beside him, with her hands behind her back and her feet apart.

A moment later Mrs. Henry sniffed the air. "What is that?" she asked.

Lou jumped and felt the back of her new dress. "I've burned a hole in it," she wailed in dismay, and then begged her mother, "What shall we do?"

Her mother comforted her distress and next day allowed her to use the family sewing machine to mend the dress and also to make a gingham sunbonnet to match.

Lou was proud of her new clothes and pleased that her

mother allowed her to help make them, but she always wanted to be like her father.

She adored her tall, broad-shouldered father. She admired his easy way of handling horses, the deft motions of his hands as he built a campfire on a weekend outing, and she listened fascinated when he explained about different kinds of rocks, trees, and flowers.

Charles Delano Henry had come by his ease in the out-of-doors naturally. His pioneer grandfather, William Henry, had helped to lay out the town of Wooster, Ohio, in 1807, interrupted several times by hostile Indians. Charles was born in Wooster. He remembered when his father became a member of the state legislature. "He was six feet tall, weighed two hundred twenty-five pounds, was smooth-shaven, and had a very dignified carriage. He was a kindly man who wore a black suit, long Prince Albert coat, and always a high silk hat," he once told Lou.

Charles Henry served for a time in the Northern army during the Civil War. When he returned from the army to Wooster, he told Phineas Weed, his father's friend, that he was determined to become a banker.

After his father's death in 1868, when Charles was twenty-three years old, he and his mother moved to Waterloo. His heart stayed in Wooster, however, for in five years he returned to marry Florence Weed, the daughter of Phineas, on June 17, 1873.

By 1874, Charles had opened the first bank in Waterloo. He was considered successful and an influential citizen. He had a beautiful young wife. In short, he had everything a man could wish for—except a son. He eagerly awaited the birth of his first child and confidently hoped it would be a boy.

It was a cold, stormy day March 29, 1874, but all was snug and warm in the spare bedroom of the house where

Florence Henry gave birth to her daughter Lou. The little newcomer was welcomed by both parents, but Florence, who knew how keenly her husband had wanted a boy, decided early to allow Charles, who loved hunting and fishing, to raise their daughter in the out-of-doors life of a boy. Always there was a strong family bond.

If at first Charles was disappointed not to have a son, he did not show it outwardly. Within a year or two his gay, active little daughter had wrapped herself around his heart completely and he could not imagine giving her up for a boy. Whenever it was possible he took her with him, no matter where he went.

By the time she was five years old Lou was allowed to go fishing with her father in a flat-bottomed rowboat on the Cedar River. On these occasions the little girl bravely learned how to tie penny-apiece fish hooks at intervals along a butcher string, while her father cut willow poles for them. "Here is your line," she would announce, "and there are six hooks on it." Angleworms for bait completed their equipment except for a sturdy jackknife, used to clean their catch before going home to the immaculate Henry kitchen.

Lou learned to ride horseback on her grandfather Scobey's [1] farm at Shell Rock. When she was six she was lifted on to a big farm horse for a bareback ride in the open fields. She loved it and begged often to return for more. As she grew taller, she rode easily, securely, and gracefully behind the high pommel of a Western saddle. She very early exhibited a love for and great skill in handling horses. By the time she was ten, she had mastered the side saddle, then rather mandatory for girls.

She first rode in a saddle with her father. She would sit sideways, with one foot resting in a sash which her father

[1] See Appendix 1 for family tree.

had looped over the saddle horn for her support. He would then mount the apron of the saddle behind her, his feet thrust into the stirrups and his arm holding the reins, passed over her shoulder to steady her. Often he would place his broad-brimmed hat on her head. He encouraged her riding and later taught her to master the wiry Western broncos, which she was allowed to ride astride like a boy, on their long trips into the hills. On the way he would describe how he had started school at the age of five and had ridden horseback a great deal until roads were improved enough to drive a buggy.

Lou paid scant attention to her dolls at this age and always preferred a game of ball or any form of play that took her out-of-doors. She went camping with her father at the tender age of six.

"We slept right on the grass," she told her mother delightedly.

"Didn't you put your canvas down first?" inquired Mrs. Henry anxiously.

"Oh, yes, and I wish we could sleep outside every night," declared Lou.

She enjoyed domestic interests, too, and this tug of war in her nature continued all her life. Florence Henry, secretly worried about her daughter's eager preference for boyish activities, resolved to teach her feminine graces and skills. Sewing was high on the list.

A girlish-looking, rather frail young woman, Mrs. Henry spent many hours in her sitting room making Christmas presents for her family. She was expert with her needle and gave Lou many ideas for little gifts, which they worked out together. Grandmother Henry was a stately woman who teasingly questioned the value of so much time spent in making Christmas "geegaws."

Everything about Lou Henry was simple and unpretentious. Even her name had no middle initial. She wore her hair bobbed because Mrs. Henry considered short hair sensible for little girls, even though it was not the height of fashion.

In those days, when "nice" girls were expected to be rather prim and sedate, a girl who liked sports was unusual, and one who liked to climb was extraordinary. No wonder Lou Henry was labeled a tomboy when she climbed up a tree at the school picnic and tied a long rope to a strong branch to provide a swing! On another occasion a student on a stepladder wrote words at the top of the schoolroom blackboard. Then the ladder was removed, but when the teacher arrived he demanded angrily that the writing be erased. Lou quickly mounted a chair, held in place on top of the teacher's desk, and erased the writing.

The father-daughter camping trips continued as Lou grew older. "Why doesn't Mama like to go camping with us?" Lou asked one day.

"This rugged kind of living doesn't agree with her," explained her father. "She wouldn't mind if she could go in a surrey and carry along a mattress to sleep on, but she really doesn't enjoy roughing it. We won't be camping so much now because pretty soon she is going to need you to help her take care of a new baby."

This realization stirred all of Lou's maternal instincts and, for the time being, she became more her mother's girl and the two talked endlessly about the coming of another child while they made baby clothes.

Lou looked forward eagerly to the arrival of the new baby and wondered if it would be a boy or a girl. Finally, the great day arrived. Lou, awakened by the commotion in her mother's room, tiptoed down the hall and was eventually admitted. She heard protesting wails and saw a wrinkled little red face in a small aperture in the swaddling clothes.

"Is it a boy or a girl?" she asked.

"This is your little sister Jean. Come and see her, darling," was the reply.

Fascinated by the newcomer, Lou loved learning how to take care of a baby and was a great help to her mother. But she continued her other interests as well, and she thoroughly enjoyed her school.

As editor of the Waterloo School paper when she was ten, she named it *Boomerang* just because she enjoyed the sound of the word—no matter what it meant. Her family surrounded her with books. She especially enjoyed nature study and history books and took a lively interest in what she read, particularly in history.

In the spring of 1884, Lou heard with some dismay that the family would be moving out West.

Lou was ten years old, a slender, blue-eyed girl, and Jean was two, when Charles and Florence Henry moved with their two daughters to Whittier, California, in search of a warmer climate for the mother of the family, and, for the father, the chance to face the challenge of starting a new bank. They went to Texas en route, and finally settled for the summer in Clearwater, Kansas, just north of the Indian Territory which later became the state of Oklahoma.

"Isn't this far enough west to go?" asked Lou.

"No," explained her father, "but this new land is filled with adventurers and many men are settling down to stay, so I promised to help open a one-man bank here before we go on to California."

"Why should we go on out there?" she persisted.

"We hope your mother's asthma will be better out

there," he replied, "and also, they need bankers in that new country."

"Will there be any horses to ride?" she wanted to know. With a quick smile he promised, "That's the first thing we will look for."

The summer in Kansas was full of interesting experiences for Lou. While she didn't have a horse to ride, a good substitute was provided in the form of a lovable, big, curly-haired bird dog which she named Logan, after a family friend. He was her constant companion as she played with baby Jean every day or took her little sister over to call upon their neighbors, the Howard Jones family.

Lou was intrigued with Mr. Jones' bicycle, which had a five-foot-high front wheel and a small rear wheel. "It would be fun," she thought, "to see him race." Characteristically, she promoted a race between Mr. Jones on his high bicycle and little Jean on her tiny velocipede, while the neighbors gathered around to cheer and Logan barked in great excitement as Jean crossed the finish line first.

Lou and Logan were permitted to explore the prairies where great open expanses were still unfenced. She often came home with wild flowers which she had picked for her mother.

"These are so pretty that we should paint them on canvas," declared Mrs. Henry as she helped Lou arrange them on the dining table. Mother and daughter spent happy hours doing water colors or oil paintings of myriads of Kansas wild flowers on Bristol board or canvas.[2] Lou often brought home pictures she had painted on any piece of tin or wood that could be found while she and Logan were exploring.

As the leaves were changing to fall colors, the Henry

2 See Appendix 2.

family boarded a Union Pacific train for three days of dusty travel to California.

The village of Whittier, founded by members of the Society of Friends, was still very young when the Henrys arrived. Only a cluster of houses lying on a slope of the foothills between the mountains and the ocean was completed in this town of 1,000 inhabitants.

"What a pretty place," exclaimed Lou, as she climbed down out of the buggy in front of 349 South Painter Avenue. She loved her new home and fairly blossomed in the friendly atmosphere of a small town, where she made friends easily and became a leader at school. But most especially, the nearness of hills and mountains to be explored excited her.

That first year, Lou walked down Painter Avenue with the other children and on through the barley fields to the country school outside the town, known as the Evergreen School.

One winter day during recess, Lou saw little Joe Anthony sobbing because he was left out of some activity. After that Lou always made sure that the only two Negro children in the school were included in the group games.

Always interested in school sports, Lou was a ringleader in clearing a vacant lot where the mustard grew tall and tough for use as a baseball diamond. She divided the volunteers into three squads of ten each. The first was to clear the space for the diamond and the other two squads about equal areas for the outfields. Lou encouraged a squad leader, "Harley Jordan, work hard now and show what you can do." There were too many spiders and tarantulas, and at first there was a threat of desertion by the workers. But Lou called out, "Never mind the spiders. They won't hurt you. But if you see any of the trap-door kind, call me. I want to catch them for my collection."

After that the work didn't stop for anything, and the boys and girls cleared nearly five acres.

Even though Charles Henry was deeply involved in problems of the bank, he found time to enjoy outings with Lou and she sensed his need of her to be his companion.

They explored the hills and rode horseback out to visit Pio Pico, the old adobe mansion of the last Mexican governor of California. Its thirty-three rooms, partially destroyed by floods in 1867, served to stimulate her interest in history, and the Henrys were quick to help their daughter find books dealing with early California days.

Lou was proud that her father was Whittier's first banker. She watched him start with one big iron safe and a simple set of books. She thought it was very pleasant to be the banker's daughter. When she walked or rode through town, grown-up men tipped their hats to her and the ladies always smiled and spoke. She knew it was because of Papa, but she liked it just the same. As she advanced in the upper grades, Lou often stopped in the bank after school. She liked the secure look of the big safe and the nice inky smell of the heavy books where Papa kept track of the money. Sometimes he let her add columns of figures for him, and then he would explain what banking was all about in such an interesting way that she had to ask question after question to find out more and more.

After the day's balances were completed, father and daughter would turn toward the open spaces. She tramped with her father through the fields and over the low hills, dressed in a hunting suit ordered especially for her from Iowa. It had a long skirt and there was a little round hat that came with it. The hat was often knocked off, so her practical mind invented rubber bands to secure it under her chin in front and to her coat collar behind.[3]

Lou and her father often took 22-caliber rifles along when they ranged through the Puente Hills because ground squirrels and gophers were a menace to crops and a nuisance to farmers. By the time Lou was thirteen she was as good a shot as her father and thought nothing of walking four or five miles every day.

During that time, one of the high spots in Lou's life was the monthly arrival of her copy of the *St. Nicholas* magazine for boys and girls. It contained stories and poems and puzzles, but among the most fascinating pages was the one that printed letters from the readers. How exciting it would be, she thought, to see your name in print. Several times she started letters, but each time she decided they weren't interesting enough and tore them up. But at last one was actually finished, sealed, and mailed. After that she watched eagerly to see if it would be printed, but month after month passed and it didn't appear. She had given up hope when one winter day she opened the magazine, turning by habit to the "Letter-box." There was her name! There was her letter! All of it. They hadn't left out a single word. She read it breathlessly.

Whittier, Cal.

Dear St. Nicholas:

Although I have taken you for nearly seven years, this is my first attempt at a letter, and I think it will have the honor of being the first sent to the "Letter-box" from Whittier, as our little town is scarcely a year old, although it has nearly a thousand inhabitants.

We think it has one of the prettiest locations possible, at the foot of the Puente Hills, about twenty miles from the

[3] See Appendix 3.

Pacific, which can be plainly seen. On clear days, we can easily count the vessels in San Pedro Harbor, twenty miles away. And the Santa Catalina Island, thirty-five miles from here, is in sight nearly all of the time. The town is 500 feet above sea level and overlooks the beautiful Los Nietos and Santa Ana valleys with their orange orchards, vineyards, etc. The hills are fifteen hundred feet above sea level, and with their lovely, although small, canyons afford splendid opportunities for picnicking and "exploring." We girls are very fond of the latter, and there are very few of the pretty spots within an afternoon's walk with which we are unacquainted. The greater portion of the inhabitants of Whittier are Friends, or Quakers; consequently the most appropriate name for the settlement was that of the great "Quaker Poet," and all true Whittierites love the name of the town almost as well as the town itself. The Friends' College, to be erected on the Pacific Coast and to cost $100,000, is located at Whittier, and the grading of the grounds for the buildings is nearly completed. The college is on quite a high hill and will be visible for miles.

"The Greenleaf" is our best hotel, and it is said to be one of the best in the southern part of the state, with exception of those in the larger cities. I am fourteen years old and my native state is Iowa, but I have also lived in Kansas and Texas. I like California best, however, for here we have only to turn around to see ocean, mountains and valley, perpetual snow and perpetual summer. I am afraid my description of the country is rather "dry," but if this is published I will write again about one of our many excursions, picnics, etc. I wish that more of your northern readers were in this land of sunshine, for I am sure that they would enjoy it as well as I do. Adios, dear St. Nicholas, with love and best wishes from your California friend and constant reader.

LOU H———.[4]

4 Published December 1887.

Her literary interests competed with athletics. A roller-skating rink became one of the main attractions for the town's children and Lou found it hard to decide whether she liked roller skating as much as she had ice skating in Iowa. But she practiced and became proficient on the rollers. During the spring of 1888 she won a contest by skating twice around the rink and blowing out nineteen candles in thirty-eight seconds. She was presented with a silk parasol for this achievement.

The next fall at school Lou portrayed the part of Joan of Arc in a class tableau. To make a coat of mail, she and a girl friend patiently snipped out enough tops of tin cans and sewed them on her sweater. They agreed it was fun to make costumes. On another occasion, Lou made herself a masquerade costume from selected pages of the town's two newspapers, the *Courier* and the *Reporter*. "I tried to use an equal quantity of each paper to show no favoritism," she said laughingly.

Lou loved to read. She was president of a schoolgirls' literary club which met at the Henry home once a week. They began their course of study with Dickens and the *Pickwick Papers* and went on to the Quaker poet, John Greenleaf Whittier, for whom the town of Whittier was named. It was here that Lou first came to know the poems of this sturdy homespun Quaker and came to know the teachings of the Society of Friends at an impressionable age.

The little town of Whittier deeply influenced Lou's life and thoughts. Sue and Bonnie, in the literary club, always went to the Quaker meetings and coaxed Lou to go with them. Lou liked the long silences in the meetings as she struggled with her own thoughts, searching for what she was and what she wanted to become. She responded naturally to the Friends' teaching of great tolerance for the beliefs and practices of other people different from herself.

She found it easy to accept the simplicity of the Friends' speech and dress and she liked the fact that women had absolute equality with men in all their meetings.

Her eager, vivid personality made her welcome in the Society of Friends, and she listened carefully to their discussions about patience, self-reliance, thrift, and personal integrity. She came to believe with them that "there is that of God in every man." This central theme of Quaker belief carried over and influenced her actions for the rest of her life as she crystallized her own convictions about the worth of every man.

From flights in religious philosophy, Lou was let down with a thud. In the big slump of the 1890s, many banks in the United States crashed. Lou was thrilled that her father was able to pull things through and that nobody lost a cent in his bank at Whittier. She was proud of his achievement, but he had to help her realize that Whittier's prosperity was finished for the time being and that there would be more challenge in Monterey. The Henrys left when it was no longer considered necessary for Whittier to maintain a bank, since so few people had money to put into one.

Those last days were difficult for Lou. She was leaving the hills and the town she loved so well and all the friends she had enjoyed so much. But in addition to this, down deep inside her she knew that she was also leaving her childhood behind.

After six years in Whittier, Charles Henry was invited by the bank in Pacific Grove to come to Monterey to start another bank. Lou was sixteen and Jean eight. They were excited to move into the big frame house at 302 Pacific Avenue, built by William Doud in 1880. "It's the biggest

house we've ever had and we will each have our own
bedroom," Lou told Jean.

Intensely curious about her new surroundings, Lou dug
into the colorful history of Monterey. At school she read
about how Juan Rodrigues de Cabrillo, a Portuguese navi-
gator in the service of Spain, sailed into Monterey Bay in
1542; how, in 1602, Sebastian Vizcaino landed there and
took possession of the country in the name of Spain. It
impressed her to learn that her sleepy little town of 1,700
people had housed the first established government in
the western United States.

Sometimes Lou rode her horse around the town exploring. She saw the old Custom House where Commo-
dore Sloat first raised the Stars and Stripes in 1846. She
and her new friends ferreted out the site of the first
theater, the first brick house, and the ancient whaling
station which was the landing place of Portola and Father
Serra.

There were luxuriant gardens around the old estates
which she visited and, loving them, she promptly began
her own garden. She was forever bringing home wild
plants to grow there.

Lou and Jean grew up in a household in which work,
recreation, and civic spirit were happily blended. Each
of the girls was assigned definite daily household tasks
which were to be completed before starting play activities. They were each given thorough instruction in sewing, cooking, and housekeeping by their mother, and encouraged to develop their skills in music and art.

Jean, who loved music, not only took violin lessons but
also found much of her recreation in musical events. Her
mother shared this liking for music, as did Lou.

Florence Henry took an active interest in her children's
school work and often visited the schoolrooms and in-

quired into the education program of the town. Her daughters' teachers were welcome guests and often warm friends in the Henry home.

It amused Lou to see what a curiosity her father was when he opened the first bank in Monterey. The people had never known a banker before and his doings were the subject of much newspaper comment. This annoyed Charles Henry and he shortly requested the editors to leave his name out of the news.

The bank of Monterey started out as a one-room institution with a heavy iron safe. As soon as there were two rooms, Lou's father, who enjoyed the human side of banking, always sat in the outer room where he could talk to the people who came in.

"A banker must keep in touch with the public," he told Lou. "I sit out here in the open to explain what a letter of credit is to a professor beginning a sabbatical leave, or outline what steps are involved in buying a house."

In her free time, Lou spent hours in the saddle exploring the whole countryside around Monterey. Her father frequently accompanied her. Writing of those days later, Lou said:

> When I was a girl in Monterey my father and I were always doing things out of doors. We would go on short hikes, or weekend camping trips, or long, exploring expeditions when we had time. We would imagine ourselves pioneers crossing the continent in covered wagons, or Father Serra and his companions in their northward pilgrimage.

In this free, joyous existence her father was her guide, philosopher, and friend. She avidly absorbed his knowledge about the structure of rocks, the varieties of birds and trees, the kinds of animals, and the need for vegetation on the hills to protect the watershed and prevent erosion.

Lou Henry grew into a slender, vital young woman, with a desire to know about all of the secrets of nature. A directness in her thinking and a quality of daring were brought out by fearless explorations of mountains, plains, and ocean. There was an irresistible appeal for her in the beauty and freedom and the scenic magnificence of the Monterey Peninsula.

At seventeen, Lou told one of her friends, "My little sister Jean is progressing with her violin and is quite a musician but I think I want to teach. Perhaps I will go to normal school next fall." She discussed plans for a teaching career with her family. "If I teach, it will have to be something about nature study," she told her mother, "maybe botany or geology."

Like all girls of her age, Lou was dreaming about her future. She knew that not too many choices of a profession were open to young women at that time. Marriage and domestic life appealed to her strongly but I would like to be able to support myself independently, she thought. Teaching was a profession open to women and Lou loved children, so normal school was a natural choice.

In the fall of 1891, Lou enrolled in the State Normal School in Los Angeles. She was elected president of her class but she stayed only one year before transferring to the San Jose Normal School. She was graduated from the latter school in the spring of 1894.[5]

There were no dormitories for students in San Jose at that time and Lou lived in a boardinghouse for girls near the campus. She delighted in telling the neighborhood children stories, usually of her own invention.

Her friends described her as having a peculiar mental and physical vitality. A bubbling-over, tireless girl, she was usually found in the midst of a group.

[5] This school later became San Jose State College.

Lou was ready for college at a time in America when the desirability of higher education for women was being debated. During the summer of 1894, when she was home from attending the normal school at San Jose, Professor John Casper Branner, head of the Department of Geology and Mines from the new Stanford University, was teaching summer science classes at Pacific Grove. An enthusiastic and inspiring man, Professor Branner gave one lecture entitled "The Bones of the Earth." Lou's imagination was fired, for she, too, knew something about those bones from her camping experiences. An animated girl, with smiling blue eyes under strongly marked eyebrows, Lou gave rapt attention to everything he said, because Professor Branner did not say the conventional things. His startling phrases and directness of speech appealed to her.

After class Lou told him about her deep interest in the earth and its structure and how she and her father had explored most of the hills around Monterey Bay from the viewpoint of a naturalist. "Do you think that a woman could study geology at Stanford?" she wanted to know.

"If you really want to study geology, Stanford is the right place," he replied, "because of the philosophy of President David Starr Jordan. Dr. Jordan said: 'The world stands aside to let any man pass who knows whither he is going. Almost every college has a great teacher. To come into contact with such a man is worth ten years of your life.' Perhaps you could find the right teacher for you at Stanford."

Lou walked home that day blind to everything but the thoughts within her. She wanted, she suddenly realized, to go to Stanford more than she had ever wanted anything before. She entered the house and hurried to find her parents.

"What is it, dear?" asked her mother.

"I want to go to Stanford," declared Lou, "and I want to study with Professor Branner and major in geology."

"But geology isn't for women, is it? Only men take it," said her mother dubiously, as she turned to her husband for confirmation.

Lou wilted.

"Your mother is right," began Charles Henry. "It would be very unusual for a girl to enter this field and you might find yourself the only girl in the classes. But what did Dr. Branner say?"

"Oh, he said I could," exclaimed Lou, her animation returning, "and I do want to study with him."

Her father understood her eagerness for geology and was proud of her ambition. When her parents finally consented, Lou went upstairs to her room and stared at herself in the mirror. Would she mind being the only girl in the classes? She would like to be married and have a home of her own. But then she remembered some of Dr. Branner's startling phrases and she knew that down deep she wanted to go to Stanford and study geology.

II

STANFORD UNIVERSITY,

COURTSHIP, MARRIAGE

•

1894–1898

BY THE TIME Lou was ready to enroll, Stanford University had been in existence for three years and there were more than eight hundred students, two hundred and fifty of them women.[1]

When Lou alighted from the Southern Pacific train she was a little apprehensive about her trunk and bags and wondered how many of the other people getting off at Palo Alto were students like herself. She was the first girl from Monterey to go to college.

"Are you going to Stanford, young lady?" asked a bronzed driver. "I have room for one more in my carriage and the boys will look after your bags."

As they rode up the palm-lined mile from the entrance gates to the college center, Lou counted thirteen buff-colored sandstone buildings with red-tiled roofs. It was exciting to reach the inner quadrangle and to see how a continuous arcade joined the one-story buildings together into a single structure surrounding an inner court.

The carriage turned toward Roble Hall, the women's

[1] See Appendix 4.

dormitory, and an upper-class student pointed out that the campus streets were named for leaders in the Spanish conquest.

"I will feel right at home with all those names here," said Lou as she read "Alvarado, Lasuen, and Salvatierra."

Most young ladies who were so advanced or so strong-minded as to go to college took the Victorianism-accepted course in English literature. But Lou Henry registered in the Department of Geology and Mining Engineering, a choice of subject which, as has been pointed out, was unheard of for a girl at that time.

In self-defense, Lou explained to one of her fellow students at Roble, "It isn't so important what others think of you as what you feel inside yourself. I love the out-of-doors and want to know how the world is made and that is what I'll learn in geology."

"Well, but don't you ever want to get married?" she was asked.

"Yes, of course. Every girl hopes for love and marriage, but I want a man who loves the mountains, the rocks, and the ocean like my father does."

"But don't you forget," persisted the questioner, "that if you know too much there will be fewer and fewer men who know more or would be interested in you?"

Torn a little by this interpretation of what nice girls were expected to take in fields of literature and language, Lou compromised and added Latin to her course. "But I don't know what I shall ever do with Latin," she mused.

On her first visit home, Lou explained to her family, "By the elective system, the students may choose all of their studies for themselves and the teacher who instructs them in their main study is supposed to coach them in the others as well. Dr. Branner will be my main teacher."

The geology department at Stanford was the center of Lou's academic interest in college, but she also loved the gymnasium. Dressed in a dark blue middy-blouse suit of serge with a four-in-hand tie, her hair braided at the back and tied with a black ribbon, she lined up eagerly with the others for military marching, club swinging, wand drills, trapeze work, and tumbling exercises. But she liked the sports best of all and entered into archery, tennis, and basketball with enthusiasm.

She often rented a horse from the livery stable in Palo Alto and she also enjoyed hiking and bicycle riding. A favorite hike was to the top of King's Mountain, a round trip of eight miles, interrupted by a ranch-house dinner at noon served by Mrs. King. On one of these trips with three couples, Lou discovered that she could easily outwalk her own escort as well as the other members of the party. She was getting acquainted with her fellow students.

Each professor knew his students well in the small classes at Stanford and an informal atmosphere reigned. Faculty "At Homes" were held on alternate Friday nights where all registered students were welcomed regardless of their major departments. No refreshments were served, but topics of the day were threshed out in lively discussions among students and faculty. Even the student literary, debating, and music clubs had some faculty members, as did all of the department clubs. Daily, while she walked from Roble Hall to her classes in the morning, Lou watched the faculty arriving from Menlo Park and Mayfield on their bicycles or from Alvarado Street on foot, all carrying their lunches.

One morning Dr. Branner dismounted from his bicycle to walk with her to the geology laboratory. He was happy because a certain senior student, who had been away on a field trip into the High Sierra, was due to return with some special rock specimens. Lou had heard the other students talk about this brilliant senior. Some were jealous of him because he was a laboratory assistant to Dr. Branner. One of the girls had told her that he was not popular but had achieved real standing with other students because he always carried through whatever projects he undertook, regardless of the difficulties encountered. She wondered what she would think of him.

That afternoon, in the geology laboratory, Lou was discussing with Dr. Branner the origin of a rock specimen when a tall, sturdy, bronzed young man walked into the room. The professor introduced Herbert Hoover to Lou Henry.

"Miss Henry thinks," he said, "that this rock belongs to the precarboniferous age. What do you think, Hoover?"

Lou was aware of hazel eyes gazing at her completely fascinated. When she returned his look, Herbert suddenly blushed, jingled the keys in his corduroy trousers pocket, and crushed his senior *sombrero* uneasily. His round face made him look immature in spite of his broad shoulders and he was tongue-tied by the introduction. What a shy, awkward boy, she thought.

She kept noticing him as they were thrown together in the geology laboratory. During the scholastic year 1894–1895 they went on frequent hikes with other students, exploring the Stanford foothills for geological formations, often accompanied by Dr. Branner, who took a lively personal interest in his students.

Lou was a new kind of girl, lithe and boyish and full of enthusiasm. When Bert Hoover, the senior in charge of the geology expedition one Saturday in November, took the crowd out on a survey he did not expect any girls.

But there was Lou, matter-of-fact and pleasant, dressed in a short skirt and sweater and sturdy walking shoes.

When they came to a ranch fence, Bert offered his hand to help her, but she did not see it. She vaulted over the fence easily and went blithely on, unconscious of difficulties. That night the boys at Encina Hall, the men's dormitory, voted their high-spirited, unflinching comrade was all right with them. From then on, Bert exhibited undue enthusiasm for taking the freshmen out on Saturday expeditions.

Bert's attitude of awed respect for Lou gradually became a friendly comradeship. This self-respecting, clear-eyed girl was a "thoroughly good fellow," the boys agreed, but not a person you would slap on the back.

On the second weekend hike, he told her a little of his background, that he had been an orphan from early childhood and had been farmed out to relatives. His elder brother Theodore and his sister May had lived with other relatives so he had grown up seeing them only at intervals. Lou knew that on the campus Bert lived in a dormitory and had earned his way during his first two years by running a laundry agency.

On another Saturday trip, Lou learned that Bert was not a good baseball player but had been highly successful as manager of the team and had raised money for equipment and uniforms which led to his present paid position of financial manager.

She found out that he was earning his way completely and that he had come to Stanford after three years of schooling at the Pacific Academy, in Newberg, Oregon, which was presided over by his uncle Dr. John Minthorn. He told her how he did chores for his uncle to pay for his keep when he was eleven years old and how he went to work for a real-estate office in Salem when he was thirteen and acquired enough schooling out of business hours to enter Stanford with a condition in English.

Lou had great respect for Bert's superior attainments in geology and, as he overcame his diffidence, she discovered that he possessed a very disarming and friendly personality. She helped him to polish up his dance steps and they attended campus parties together all winter long, but never fraternity affairs, since Bert was opposed to the "Greeks" as being undemocratic.

Greek-letter fraternities had been established on the campus, and they helped to solve the housing problem for students who could afford to live in them. The student body tended to divide politically and socially into the Greeks and non-Greeks or Barbarians.

Lou knew her own mind in social matters, as well as in her choice of professional training. She was pledged to the Kappa Kappa Gamma sorority and was, therefore, classed on campus as a "Greek."

During the winter, Lou and Bert often strolled the campus paths together through the cactus garden or under the eucalyptus trees where they discussed more personal subjects than rock formations. They discovered that they were both born in Iowa the same year and only fifty miles apart, and also that they both came West about the same time.

"Why does Lou go walking with Herbert Hoover, that 'barbarian' engineering student?" asked one of her sorority sisters, "when she could have half-a-dozen men in the frats?"

By spring, these two young people were inseparable on the long geology field trips which provided more opportunity to get acquainted. Lou and Bert chipped off specimens of rock with hammers and sat on ledges in the sunshine to examine them. She made it easy for him to talk about his hopes, ambitions, and plans. He told her how his father had died of typhoid when he was only six and his mother of pneumonia when he was ten. Lou heard about the four generations of Friends in his family and about his own strong Quaker faith and his deep desire to serve his country and his God. Under blue California skies, the friendship of the senior and freshman blossomed into an enduring romance.

A girl chum at Roble Hall declared, "Bert used to come to see some of us before he met Lou, but now he doesn't know there is another girl on the campus."

The end of the school year was filled with social activities, and Lou was regularly accompanied by Bert. At the Senior Ball, she danced with him in the gymnasium where pepper boughs and bamboo screened the basketball hoops and other permanent apparatus which was on the walls. She knew that he was worried about financing their attendance at the Senior Ball but didn't learn until long afterward that he had borrowed the necessary $7.50 from his brother Theodore, a linotype operator for the Oakland *Tribune.*

The pair met the next evening for the graduation exercises in the old quad, which was lighted with rosy lanterns. Against these colored balloons of light, freshman Lou walked through the arches in her long, fluffy white dress that rippled in soft foam at her feet, not heeding that the orchestra was playing "Auld Lang Syne." With three more years to go, her life at Stanford was just beginning, but not so for graduate Herbert Hoover. Presently she heard him, choked with emotion, ask, "Will you write to me?"

Clear-eyed and frank, she answered, "Of course I will." Intuitively she recognized, "This is all he can ask me now,

because he thinks he has nothing to offer; as if that mattered."

A more or less definite engagement existed when they
parted that evening, but she recognized his possessive,
driving interest in his own professional career and,
secretly, she began to wonder if he would have room in
his life for a wife.

Lou Henry was proud of Herbert Hoover when he received his diploma which read "Bachelor of Arts in Geology," and had every confidence that he would soon land
an important engineering job. She knew that they shared
the same enthusiasms for geology and love of wide-open
spaces. She admired his ability and courage as she thought
back on how this orphan boy had forged ahead and made
his own way. She could subscribe wholeheartedly to his
personal philosophy and religious views. That she would
eventually marry him was an easy decision and it pleased
her when her friends agreed that they were well matched.

She was interested to meet Bert's brother, who came
to Palo Alto to attend the graduation. Bert told her that
Theodore had rented an apartment on Ellsworth Street,
in Berkeley, to be shared by the two brothers and their
sister May.

During her summer vacation, Lou invited some of her
Stanford schoolmates to visit her and reveled with them
on long walks in the woods, visits to Carmel and Monterey
missions, and trips to Del Monte and Pacific Grove. They
wore old-fashioned sunbonnets and carried tin pails to
collect huckleberries as they rode over the hills or went
fishing up the Carmel River. Occasionally they went to
one of the picturesque Monterey restaurants for an elaborate Spanish dinner.

"Why doesn't Bert come down?" her house guests asked
her.

"He has to earn his own living," she replied, "and this summer he has to help support his sister, too. You know their parents died a long time ago."

The next three years were busy but lonely for Lou. During her sophomore and junior years at Stanford, she saw Bert only a few times. Once he told her his first job in the Reward Mine at Nevada City had been a big disappointment in mining experience and paid very little besides.

"That was the life of an earthworm, crawling in the darkness, accomplishing nothing, learning nothing, just piling up ore for the mills. Is this what four years of college is worth?"

His job had consisted of shoveling a wet mixture of dirt and ore into a push car at the bottom of a mine. But he did learn how to get along with the Cornish miners and all the tricks of the trade at an underground level of a mine. A little later he took samples of ore, checked veins, discussed mining problems with the manager, and combined his new store of practical mining knowledge with his geology. He was learning more than he realized at the time. This combination of the practical with the theoretical opened many doors for him in the years to come.

Before long, the girls from the Kappa Kappa Gamma house talked about the letters Lou received from Colorado, Nevada, Wyoming, Idaho, Arizona, and New Mexico, as the young engineer was sent out on geological surveys of many mines.

On a quick trip home from New Mexico, Bert told Lou about the white heat, sand and sagebrush, Mexican huts, naked brown babies, water jugs carried on the saddle, gamblers, saloons, promoters, and brawling in the mining country. She learned that as he moved rapidly from one assignment to another he was filling every spare minute of time with omniverous reading on many subjects.

"Geology is fun," he told her, "but it is mostly knowledge for its own sake. Mining, on the other hand, is the application of our knowledge of geology to the practical affairs of men. And now I have to choose between the two. If I choose the latter, do you think you could go to the ends of the earth with a mining engineer?"

"Of course I could," she agreed, and felt little shivers of excitement at the thought.

Lou was confident that he would do well as a mining engineer because he had an unusual faculty for organization and because, with Quaker integrity, he always held high his regard for the dignity and ethics of his profession.

She thought about her early years with the Quakers in Waterloo and how she had responded to the teachings of the Friends in Whittier. So it was easy for her to share Bert's Quaker ideals and beliefs. She discussed this matter with Theodore, who had enrolled at Stanford that year as a freshman.

The end of her senior year was gay with parties for Lou and her sorority sisters. Many romantic revelations were made on these occasions but Lou waited for her disclosure until graduation week when her mother, father, and sister Jean arrived. Then at a special dinner party at the Kappa house, Lou announced that she planned to marry Bert Hoover as soon as he had a job that would keep him in one place long enough to make a home.

Announcement of their engagement made quite a stir at Stanford. Mrs. Branner was surprised. "I thought they were just pals," she said. "Lou hasn't gone in for love affairs and would rather tramp around the hills than do anything else."

"We have yet to meet this roving young man," explained Mrs. Henry. "We hoped he would be here for Lou's commencement."

Lou particularly enjoyed showing Jean around the campus, but on graduation day her thoughts turned toward her future life with a certain mining engineer and living in faraway places.

On her graduation day in the spring of 1898, Lou was described by Professor Branner as one of Stanford's most highly esteemed young women and a good student, although no grades were given. At that time, students received only a plus for passing or a minus for failing.

After graduation, Lou returned to Monterey where she was immediately called upon to replace a teacher who had resigned before the end of the year to be married. Because the school building had burned, Miss Lou Henry met her classes in a little social hall rented by the trustees from the Catholic church. Every day she saw the young parish priest, Father Ramōn Mestres, who had recently come from Barcelona, Spain, and promptly became the friend and loving caretaker of a large part of the population of the town. He was particularly interested in history and in the social institutions of his church. He helped to organize a recreational program in the town and Lou and her father often played tennis with him. After classes were over, Miss Henry's Catholic pupils went to Father Mestres for religious instruction, while she ran home to check the mail.

These were months of making plans with Bert by letter. From London, Lou heard that her fiancé had been offered a big opportunity in Australia, where he would be on his own in developing a mine and have a chance to be successful. They planned that he would return to California on his first vacation, so that they could be married. He told her he was now earning enough so that he could repay all the money he had borrowed from his brother and, in addition, loan enough to help finance Theodore's last two years at Stanford.

Letters soon began arriving from Bert postmarked Kalgoorlie, in the hot desert interior of Australia, where he was developing the Sons of Gwalia gold mine (which remained in continuous operation for the succeeding fifty years).

One of these letters brought exciting information. "Bert thinks he may go to China," Lou told her mother. "The Boy Emperor, Kwang Hsu, is ambitious for China to develop Western industrial methods to meet European competition in trade. He is bringing in foreign technical advisers to help with his 'reform' projects."

"China!" gasped Mrs. Henry. "How could he ever go there?"

Lou's eyes danced with excitement as she explained. "Bert has been offered the job of chief engineer for this Chinese engineering and mining company. He says they want a man no more than thirty years old but with seventy-five years' experience." She twinkled. "He thinks the job is too big for him, but he wants the chance to try it."

"When will he go?" asked Mrs. Henry.

"Probably very soon," replied Lou, "and he wants me to go with him."

Ten days later, Lou, looking out a window, saw the telegraph boy from the Monterey office on his bicycle pedaling rapidly toward the Henry home. She ran out to meet him. It was a cable from Bert proposing a wedding date with a honeymoon trip to China. Lou was delighted.

Some of her friends were aghast. "How can you possibly go to China?" they asked. "That is no place for a white woman to live. You will have to eat bird's-nest soup and learn to use chopsticks and they don't have beds to sleep on either."

Lou's color mounted, partly from her own excitement but partly in indignation as she declared heatedly, "Bert will need a home no matter where he is going to work and I will help him wherever he goes."

After this outburst, Lou walked upstairs to her own room to be alone with her thoughts, which were in a jumble of excitement, trepidation, and pleasurable anticipation of the future, but mixed with a few doubts. Deep inside her she wanted to establish a permanent, secure home of their own, but most of all she wanted to help Bert with his career and be a loyal, venturesome wife.

Bert hurried to California from Australia as quickly as he could, but he had to go by way of London to make a report to the Bewick, Moreing Company, his employers, on the Kalgoorlie Mine. It was five weeks after Lou received his cable that he finally arrived in Monterey, on January 31, 1899. The neatly-groomed and deeply-bronzed young man could not take his eyes off his fiancée as they rode in the Henry family carriage to her home. Lou, supremely happy, presented him proudly to her family in the serene old house among the pepper trees and roses. Charles Henry, dignified but friendly, sought composure by looking at his wife who was trying to smile a warm welcome as she contemplated losing her daughter to this dynamic young man who was en route to China.

Jean liked Bert instantly and told her parents, "You know you are not losing a daughter, you are gaining a son and I am getting a brother." Then she was off to tell her girl friends about the wedding.

There were only ten days in which to plan the wedding and show Bert around picturesque Monterey.

Lou had wanted to exchange vows with Bert in the

approved Quaker fashion in a Friends' Meeting, but there was no Quaker colony near Monterey. It happened that, for a few days, there was no Protestant minister in the town either.

"We can't postpone it," Lou told her parents, "because Bert has a travel deadline to meet, so why not call Father Mestres? Do you think he would need a special dispensation?"

"No," answered her father, "because he performs many Protestant marriages in his capacity as a civil magistrate."

Lou was eager to have Bert see the places she loved so well in Monterey and to say a little "good-bye" to them for herself. "Don't you love these quaint tiled adobe houses of the old Spanish capital?" she asked him. "Look at the orange and fig trees in the yards and the paths bordered with those colorful abalone shells." They explored the shops and the quiet streets, and they walked along lonely miles of white beaches watching the tiny white-breasted sandpipers scampering along in the scallops made by the foam.

There were long talks with the family around the fireplace in the evenings. Lou was proud of the adroit way that Bert tried to allay any fears that Charles and Florence Henry had about the hazards of life in China and how quickly he responded to all of Jean's questions.

"We will be living in a big port city where there are lots of other Americans," he explained, stretching his feet toward the hearth. "Lou knows all about how unpredictable the career of a mining engineer is bound to be, but she wants to go with me, anyway," and he flashed her an appreciative smile.

As Lou watched the fire, she remembered how people were gossiping about her dangerous journey. But what fleeting fears she had herself were more than counterbalanced by the joyful anticipation she had for the adventures they would share as she accompanied Bert into the dubious interior of China.

"It looks as though it will be an ideal marriage," Charles Henry confided to his wife. "They are perfect partners, comrades, and friends. Also, she is physically fit to rough it a little bit and is intellectually able to discuss his professional problems with him."

Plans for the wedding went forward. Jean was to play her violin and was practicing passionately. Bert's sister May and his brother Theodore were to come down from Berkeley for the occasion. The Henrys arranged for the mission padre, their family friend, to perform the ceremony at the Henry home on Pacific and Jackson streets. Lou lived in happy excitement.

Finally the day arrived, bringing a blue sky with sunbeams dancing through the bougainvillaea vine on the front porch. The house was filled with flowers. Only the immediate family and a few friends were present for the wedding.

Father Mestres, in his long black robe, stood with the bridegroom. Bert, with his straight hair carefully parted in the middle and dressed in a new brown suit, was wearing a high white collar that seemed to bother him. They stood watching the door of the sitting room as Lou came in on her father's arm. She wore a brown travel suit with a double-breasted jacket open over a lovely white Russian blouse. Her tailor-made English skirt was nearly ankle length.

Since the Henrys were Episcopalians, there were elements of three faiths in the wedding ceremoney as Lou Henry and Herbert Hoover joined hands and mutually repeated their wedding vows, Quaker fashion.

The young couple were married at high noon on Friday,

February 10, 1899. They left for San Francisco at two
o'clock. En route, in Palo Alto, there was a gathering of
Lou's college friends at the station, armed with rice and
old shoes. Bert chuckled as his special friend, Ray Lyman
Wilbur, dashed up in a car and climbed aboard the moving train, while Lou stood in the rear doorway kissing her
hands to the crowd.

The townspeople of historic Monterey maintained old
Spanish traditions of many assorted festivities incident to
a wedding. They gasped for breath at the suddenness
with which the young engineer arrived from Australia by
way of London, married the lovely daughter of the town's
banker, and departed with her for China, all in such
a few days.

Charles and Florence Henry with Jean, Theodore and
May Hoover, went to San Francisco on Saturday to watch
the happy couple embark.

Saturday, February 11, was another one of those perfect days. San Francisco Bay was as blue as the sky above
and Goat Island stood out in clear detail. At the pier, all
was bustle and excitement as the hands of the wharf
clock pointed to twelve. It was a happy throng of people
who stood watching the big ship pulling out. A rainbow
cloud of paper streamers tied a multitude of outstretched
hands together across the little expanse of water, and one
by one the colored streamers snapped as the distance between the ship and pier widened.

Lou held the paper ribbons connecting her to her father,
her mother, and her sister Jean. As one by one her ribbons
snapped, the new Mrs. Hoover wondered how long it
would be until she would see them again. The ship's
orchestra played the traditional "Aloha Oe, Farewell to
Thee," and Lou could see her mother dabbing her eyes

with a handkerchief. Then Bert took her arm firmly and her thoughts turned toward her future with him.

"Let's explore the ship," he suggested.

The Hoovers had set sail for China loaded down with all the books about the Orient that they could buy. During the three-and-a-half-week honeymoon trip across the Pacific, the young couple absorbed together much information about Chinese life and customs.

On shipboard they started an enduring friendship with Frederick Palmer, war correspondent, and his wife. At the dinner table they had much conversation with William Rockhill, secretary of the United States Legation in Peking, and with an interesting missionary pair, Dr. and Mrs. W. A. Staley, who were returning to Shensi Province. They discussed the Boer War, which was starting in South Africa, and bemoaned a growing imperialism in the world.

III

EXPERIENCES IN CHINA

•

1899–1901

It was march when the ship, with the young Hoovers aboard, docked at the Tong Ku wharf, in the mouth of the Pei River on the outskirts of Tientsin where ocean-going vessels were unloaded.

Lou and Bert climbed into rickshas and rode a couple of miles through a densely populated suburb, en route to the main part of Tientsin, the most important commercial city in North China. Lou noted with concern how the coolies strained at the ropes across their raw shoulders as they pulled the heavy boxes of cargo taken from the ship through the streets in squeaking Peking carts. She marveled at how the ricksha boys darted in and out through the heavy traffic on the narrow streets without colliding.

Finally the two Americans reached the foreign settlement, which consisted of an area eight to ten blocks long on three parallel streets. On one side lay the Pei River and on the other an open field. The couple stayed overnight at the Astor House, a hotel in the foreign settlement, and the next day traveled by train fifty miles northeast to

Peking, where they went immediately to the American consulate.

There ensued much discussion among the Chinese officials as to the proper housing for the new chief engineer in charge of the mines for the Chinese government. It was finally decided that the Hoovers should live in the foreign settlement in Tientsin.

Herbert Hoover's main job was to discover the extent and boundaries of the deposits in the large Tongshan and Kaiping coal fields, near Tientsin. But Chang Yen-mao, the Imperial Commissioner of Mines, wanted him to discover gold mines. Chang also held the position of Director-General of the government's engineering and mining company, which had hired the young American, and consequently the Commissioner took Bert out on a number of trips over North China, in search of gold.

For the first few weeks, the Hoovers stayed at the Astor House, in the foreign settlement, and Lou pored over books and reports and planned to work out and map the geology of the region. In the evenings, she enjoyed walking through the lantern-lighted streets of the city with Bert. They smelled the pungent incense coming from the temples, listened to the strange wailing and crashing of a new kind of music, and watched the great dragon parade. The shops opened directly on narrow streets crowded with sedan chairs, rickshas, and trotting coolies. She stopped often to look at multicolored silks displayed, the varieties of embroidery, the carved jewels, the heavily varnished paper parasols, and the many new foods.

Lou immediately started looking for a house where she could make a home for Bert. In the meantime, he rented a big house on Racecourse Road and established the American Engineers' Club, with assayers' offices downstairs and living quarters upstairs for the American engineers who had joined him for work in the Chinese mines.

Finally Lou found just what she wanted, a little farther up on the same street. It was a blue brick house, built Western style, with a tile roof and a wide veranda.

I can make a comfortable home here, she thought and began to inquire about hiring servants.

"In Tientsin, I encountered the oriental 'squeeze' system of sharing this world's goods," Lou told her friends later, "and the highly technical 'union lines' observed by Chinese servants within a household. No foreign woman in the Orient tries to do her own marketing for food, partly because of language difficulty and partly because all food 'squeeze' belongs by right to the cook."

According to the established custom, Lou arranged to "board with the cook." She had to specify what foods were to be served at the various meals and agree to pay the cook a set sum of money. What he could squeeze out of the agreed-upon price was his profit. The houseboy and amah (woman servant) kept the house clean, while the ricksha boys ran the "chits" or notes which substituted for a telephone. They also pulled the Hoovers' private rickshas. The gardener kept up the grounds. A servant of one category would not be caught performing any of the duties of another category. Prevailing wages paid to servants in the Orient were so low that the employment of six servants did not represent a financial burden for the newly married couple.

To furnish her house, Lou Hoover found some chairs and tables were available for rent from the company godowns or warehouses, but she had to have the bedsteads and dish cupboards made by local artisans, who copied pictures of the desired furniture. This was a slow process and was also involved in various legitimate "squeezes."

In going from shop to shop looking for household equipment, Lou became interested in antique Chinese porcelains and eventually built up a fine collection of blue-and-white Ming and K'ang Hse sets.[1] But she settled for the vitreous, more or less translucent ceramic ware of local manufacture for the Tientsin house. These dishes were readily available in the local shops. The cups had neither handles nor saucers, and deep round rice bowls were of chief importance in serving a Chinese meal.

The blue house quickly became a home under the direction of the young wife, who seemed to possess that special natural ability. She opened their hospitable doors often to Bert's lonely young engineers and she made friends quickly in the foreign settlement. She especially enjoyed Mrs. Edward Drew, wife of the Commissioner of Customs, and often went shopping with her.

Accepted by the diplomatic set, the Hoovers met many prominent people and became accustomed to the usages of official entertaining. The friendly, unpretentious Lou was irked at the precisely defined social scale among the few foreign residents and the highly conventionalized social life of the foreign colony, and made a special point of keeping her own entertaining simple and informal. Entertaining was part of her job as a wife, but she also gave Bert some technical help with his.

The Hoovers plunged into their professional work with great zest. Bert examined ore by day and he and his wife studied mining laws at night. She helped in the collecting, translating, and summarizing of all the literature available on Chinese mining, and then, with her technical education and understanding, took over cataloging the mining laws of the world, for Bert to give to Chang Yen-mao.

[1] Some of these pieces are on display in the Hoover Institution at Stanford University.

There was much to write home about and they also watched for letters from America. Mail brought the news that May Hoover was married to Van Ness Leavitt in March and that Theodore married Mildred Brooke of Baltimore in June.

Lou was eager to see China and went on a number of trips into the countryside with Bert. She rode shaggy Manchurian ponies along impossible roads while guards went ahead to protect the Americans against bandits. Sometimes the Hoovers camped out, but more often they were lodged at native inns. These were bare one-story rooms, surrounding an open courtyard. She watched the servants as they spread plaited grass mattresses and bedding on top of a kang or brick shoulder of the fireplace. After preparing dinner from the packs, the servants lighted a tiny charcoal blaze in the fireplace in the Hoovers' quarters to keep the kang warm all night.

The neighboring Chinese children crowded around early in the mornings to catch their first glimpse of a white woman. In the village shops, Lou learned to recognize the blue-and-white Ming porcelain which she loved and collected when she could.

She watched the coolies working in the millet fields in the north and visited crowded villages of adobe houses with straw-thatched roofs. She saw a country swarming with millions of people living in squalor, patiently clinging without complaint to the precarious edge of starvation.

"How much longer will they endure it?" she asked Bert.

"They have never dreamed of better things," he replied.

On one trip into Shensi Province, Lou contracted a severe cold, so she stayed in the mission compound of their shipboard friends, the Staleys, for several weeks while Bert went into the interior with Chang Yen-mao.

Lou told her hostess that Bert was a little discouraged with Chang's search for gold.

"The Chinese expect Bert to look down on the land from a hilltop and tell them where to dig for gold. But they do not accept his suggestions about a more honest work day or cutting the payroll by removing the 30 percent of fictitious names."

"Perhaps they consider these things are all part of their legitimate squeeze," suggested Mrs. Staley.

While living a life of unaccustomed inactivity among the rural Chinese, Lou had many discussions with Mary Staley about the silent, unresisting, unconquerable inertia of China. When Bert returned and took her back to Tientsin, she told him, "I have decided that I need a great deal more Chinese language study to help me understand these people."

She was able to hire a highly recommended teacher and started studying the language systematically, sitting opposite the bearded Chinese sein sen (teacher) for a couple of hours each morning learning how better to direct her household and to shop. With her new vocabulary, she later acquired a rare collection of books on China.

From her teacher, Yueh-tung Chuan, she learned much of the philosophy of China where pushing and hurrying had no place. "Why hurry?" he asked, and told her this proverb:

> The river of the centuries passes slowly. There have been 10,000 times 10,000 years. There will be 10,000 times that number. One man is a snowflake on the ocean of time; his affairs are of no moment. We live, we will die, others will come after us living and dying. Let us be calm.

Yueh-tung Chuan had taught many foreigners and he was much impressed with Lou. When she presented a gift to his family, he said, "You are a good pupil and your kind manner and humble attitude will always be remembered by me. I hope we shall long be friends."

Lou proved to be an apt student and soon had sufficient command of the Chinese language to be able to travel much more easily. Mrs. Drew urged her to explore Peking thoroughly, so she told Bert, "We should plan several trips to Peking while we are so close." He readily agreed.

One Saturday they took their lunches and decided to get a bird's-eye view of the city. They had to start early in the morning to hike around the fourteen miles on top of Peking's outer enclosing wall.

"Bert, did you read how the Mings built the present wall in 1420 A.D.?" asked Lou. "How tall is it?"

"At least forty feet high and as broad on top as any downtown street at home," he answered.

They climbed up to the top of the city wall at the Chien Men or front gate and looked down on the ceaseless traffic below. The quietness up there was almost unbelievable. Barefoot or sandle-shod coolies straining at heavy loads or pulling rickshas made only soft thuds with their feet. On top of the wall, only the sound of their voices in rhythmic "hai ya ho," the song of the burden bearers, or the sharp calling of "wei wei chei tze lai," clear the way for the ricksha men, could be heard. The city's daily food was pouring in through the gate. There were small mule-drawn, covered Peking carts, the constant creak of their solid wheels muffled. There were droves of donkeys trotting through the gate, urged on by men in rough country dress. But most picturesque were the long strings of camels that made their leisurely way noiselessly as they brought in their loads of coal from across the Gobi Desert.

"Why do they look so moth-eaten?" Lou wanted to know.

"That is because every time they stop the camel drivers pluck off all the loose hair and keep it in those bags that they carry," explained Bert. "They use it to make rugs."

"Can you possibly imagine any greater contrast to the constant din of a busy city street in America having the same volume of traffic?" asked Lou.

When they could get away from the fascination of looking at the streets below, they started on their hike. The plan of the four cities that made up Peking was plainly visible from where they were, and they could see walls within walls. Bert said, "The North City looks like a big box enclosing two smaller ones. The Forbidden City is that smallest central box, easily distinguished by its yellow tile roofs."

"Isn't it interesting that the life within the Forbidden City is set apart from the life of the people as is the area itself?" asked Lou.

"Yes," agreed Bert, "and the next larger box is the Imperial City, the aristocratic residential district, where many of the officials live."

Outside this and forming a third and still larger box were the walls of the Tartar or Manchu City. Lou and Bert were swinging along at a good pace by now.

"There must be something about this Peking air that is stimulating," commented Lou, "for I feel as light as a bird."

South of the Tartar City they saw the Chinese City where the common people lived, enclosed in a box of its own. The southern wall of the Tartar City was part of the northern wall of the Chinese City and from there they looked down on the shops.

"Mrs. Drew and I have been down there shopping already and we won't be able to pay our board to the cook if we go again," confessed Lou.

A little way beyond the Hatamen, or Gate of Sublime Learning, they came to the observatory. "Look at those queer old bronze astronomical instruments decorated with dragons," exclaimed Lou, "and see how discolored with age they are."

The guide at the observatory told them that the Chinese followed a Persian system of astronomy as far back as A.D. 1280, and the observatory was built by Kublai Khan about that time.

"It certainly makes us Americans sound very young and very presumptuous to be teaching the Chinese," commented Bert.

Weekends found the young people busy with trips to the many points of interest about Peking. With characteristic thoroughness, Lou had insisted that they read up on the history and mythology of each place to be visited before setting out. The famous Temple of Heaven was one of the first major objectives.

They enjoyed visiting this shrine because they knew it was one of the few remaining evidences of the very early Chinese worship of the unseen god. They were both impressed by the Altar of Heaven itself. In the center of the enclosure belonging to the temple they saw a pure-white marble platform with no roof, perfectly round and rising in three tiers. In the center of the third and highest platform was a round block of purest white marble on which was set the shrine to Shang Ti, the unseen god.

"The center of this altar is the center of the universe," declared their priest guide, "and therefore China is called 'Chung Kuo,' or central kingdom.

"The most beautiful building in all Peking," continued

the guide, "is the Temple of Heaven a little north of the altar."

Soon they saw a gorgeous blue tile roof. The building was circular, had a triple roof, and stood on a three-tiered marble terrace. Their guide told them it was 99 feet high and that the three roofs were supported by lacquered columns made of huge logs of Oregon pine, brought over from the United States in 1890 when the temple was rebuilt after a fire. They saw phoenixes and dragons of gold and many colors painted on the ceiling, and windows resplendent with elaborate carved wooden screens and fancy brass hinges.

Lou loved these sight-seeing jaunts with her husband, especially since so many of his journeys were to inaccessible interior places where the mode of travel made it impossible for her to go along. However, one trip was different. It was to be by boat.

"How would you like to see the dikes along the Yellow River?" Bert Hoover asked his wife. "The Yangtze is the biggest river in China, but the basin of the Hwang Ho is more important to agriculture. It is 3,000 miles long and is called the Yellow River because it carries so much silt. The river has changed its course many times to cause catastrophe. I told Li Hung-chang, head of the Yellow River Commission, that I am not a flood-control expert, but he has insisted that I go and examine the dikes anyway."

The next day Lou climbed aboard a square-nosed river junk with multi-patched sails and started with her husband on the inspection trip of the flood-control works of the Hwang Ho.

"Fearful loss of life results nearly every year when the Hwang Ho breaks out of its dikes," Bert told her. "The country people refer to it as the 'sorrow of China' and believe that the ruling dynasty can stay in power only as long as the dikes hold."

The inspection trip by boat made it apparent to Bert that the engineering was fairly good, but that the upkeep was poor and there was much need of repairs. They learned that whenever the ruling dynasty became corrupt the annual appropriations for the dikes disappeared into the pockets of unscrupulous politicians.

Bert told Lou privately, "Now I begin to understand the origin of the so-called 'superstitions' about the dikes and the fall of the ruling dynasty."

Interesting as the river was, Lou looked forward to another trip to Peking because the capital city was always irresistible to her. In early June 1900 she went there with Bert to do some more sight-seeing, while he crossed the Great Wall to inspect a mine farther north.

Upon her return, Lou told Mrs. Drew, "While I was riding in a ricksha, a severe dust storm came up and I thought that the Gobi Desert was descending upon me. I couldn't breathe. I was really sick and genuinely relieved when Bert returned and had me carried to the train. My own doctor here in Tientsin found that I had a bad sinus infection."

This was Lou Hoover's last trip to Peking. Moving about became increasingly difficult because with the beginning of anti-foreign demonstrations, the ricksha men refused to serve white people. A great wave of hatred of Caucasians was spreading over China, actively supported by the Empress Dowager. Herbert Hoover, of course, represented a British firm.

The Boy Emperor, Kwang Hsu, had issued his series of proclamations in 1898 to announce his intention to bring in experts from other nations in an attempt to reorganize China along modern lines. But the very shrewd Empress

Dowager dethroned the young Emperor, by means of palace intrigue, and succeeded in creating the impression that all the ills of China were owing to the foreigners who had come to help in the reorganization at the invitation of Kwang Hsu. She instigated the Boxer Rebellion, led by fanatically "patriotic" Chinese who were bent upon wiping out the "foreign devils."

The vengeful Chinese were called Boxers. In their fury, they killed 250 missionaries and other foreigners in the interior of northeastern China, along with nearly 30,000 Chinese Christians. The foreign settlements in Peking and Tientsin were among the first targets of the Boxers.

News that the legations in Peking were under siege came like a thunderclap to Lou and Bert Hoover. International troops marched through the streets of Tientsin going to their rescue, and vanished in the north. The Hoovers had been home from Peking for only a few days before that Sunday morning, June 10, 1900, when they were rudely awakened by shells bursting over their compound and found themselves engulfed in the Boxer Rebellion.

"You had better cable our families at home that we are safe so they won't worry," Bert advised Lou, "and then we will get you down-river to the Tong Ku port under the protection of American and British warships."

"You know I won't go without you," she replied firmly. She stood close to him on the roof of the Engineers' Club and watched the fires beyond the walls of the city that marked the burning missions. "They won't dare attack the foreign settlement. The Empress Dowager wouldn't defy the whole world," she reasoned.

"Don't be too sure," replied her husband.

The anti-foreign feeling involved the household help. As the days went by most of the servants disappeared.

Two, however, remained loyal to Lou. The Hoovers had grown used to hearing gunfire to the north and there were many missionaries and teachers arriving continually at the foreign settlement in Tientsin seeking refuge.

One afternoon, as Lou was sitting in her garden still recuperating from her recent sinus infection, she heard shooting close at hand. Rifle bullets began crashing into the brick compound walls surrounding the Hoover house. Bert hurried home from the assayers' office to break the appalling news that most of the Chinese army had suddenly gone Boxer.

"The exhausted white officers in charge of training the Imperial troops barely escaped being killed," he told his wife. "Friendly Chinese officers warned them just in time."

He added, with a catch in his voice, "I shouldn't have let you stay."

Standing on the roof of their house, they saw through their field glasses the Chinese army that was attacking and they heard the screams of shells overhead. Bert groaned, "See what I've brought you to."

Her clear blue eyes held a steady light in them as she assured him, "It's all right, I'm glad that you did. A year and three happy months together. I tell you I'm glad. Glad, whatever happens."

The Hoovers were aware of the dangerous situation of their house, which was located at the end of the street nearest to the Chinese armies. It was, perhaps, the most conspicuous target in the foreign settlement. Edward Drew and his family occupied a large house surrounded by a strong wall within the inner circle of the settlement. He offered hospitality to the Hoovers and any others who lived in exposed places.

"I'll take our bedding over to Lucy Drew's home on my

bicycle," said Lou, "and then our two servants can help run her household."

The Drew home became an American dormitory, with the women sleeping on the floor in one big room and the men in another. Lou took charge of the food rationing and planned the meals and the Drews' coolie did the cooking.

The 300 able-bodied men in the foreign settlement formed a home guard and assigned for themselves rotating sentry duty and various police, ambulance, and engineering responsibilities. Bert directed the building of a strong barricade on the most exposed side of the settlement, using sugar barrels and bags of grain taken from the godowns or warehouses within the area. He directed his special attention toward protecting the water supply.

In the actual military defense of Tientsin, the fighting was done by approximately 2,500 soldiers, representing eight nations in the foreign settlement.

Every afternoon Lou took hot tea to the home-guard defenders behind the barricade of sugar barrels. "They need it to hearten them and help take their minds off their grim business," she said. She also took her turn in the small compound at the Drew home watching for fires that might be started by bullets. With unshakable poise and courage, Lou Hoover helped wherever she could throughout the long month that the compound was besieged. Before a hospital was organized, she pedaled her bicycle around the compound, gathering bed sheets to be used as bandages for the wounded people. There was incessant artillery fire from the Boxers, answered by the defenders, and many were wounded. Soon, two army doctors and a nurse turned the clubhouse into a hospital.

One morning, after sweeping spent bullets off her front porch, Lou rode her bicycle to the hospital. I can use my old woodcraft technique and avoid being struck by stray shells, she thought. Just then, one of her bicycle tires was punctured by a bullet, so she walked on to the hospital to help nurse the wounded.

Dozens of Allied soldiers were brought into the club-house every day with gunshot wounds. The temporary hospital was short of everything—cots, bedding, bandages —and Lou begged the occupants of stores and houses for still more supplies.

After three weeks, the besieged people in the foreign settlement heard that the Great Powers were sending in troops to relieve them. American and Japanese soldiers were coming from the Philippines, British from Shanghai, and French from Indo-China.

The first relief contingent was accompanied by four American war correspondents: Oscar King Davis of the New York *Sun,* Robert Collins of Associated Press, Frederick Palmer of *Collier's,* and Joaquin Miller, the irrepressible California poet of the Hearst Syndicate. They needed a place to stay. While browsing about in search of supplies for the hospital, Lou had observed that their house was no worse off than the others in the foreign settlement. So the Hoovers moved back to their own home and invited the correspondents to be their guests.

One evening as Lou and Bert sat on their porch, a shell shattered a light overhead. "It is getting a little noisy out here," remarked Lou. "Maybe we should move inside."

"You're pretty plucky," admired her husband.

The next afternoon, while the war correspondents were working on their dispatches in their rooms, a shell brought down the Japanese sentry at their compound gate. Since the gate was quite a distance from the house, Lou, who had been playing solitaire in the downstairs library, walked upstairs to see what had happened. There was nothing to be seen but the back of the gatehouse so she returned to her game, not knowing of their loss until the next day when she went to the hospital.

Ten minutes later, a much closer explosion came as a shell burst through their upper back window and destroyed a post at the head of the stairs. The correspondents rushed down through the mortar dust and smoke to find Lou calmly turning over her cards. "I don't seem to be winning this game," she said, "but that was the third shell and therefore the last one for the present anyway. Their pattern is three in a row." Neatly stacking her cards, she invited, "Let's go and have tea."

Finally, late in July, more Allied troops, including additional American and British, plus some Germans and Russians, came marching through the streets and the siege was over. After another week there were enough relief troops to protect the escape roads and the women and children in the foreign settlement were evacuated to Shanghai. Most of the men left, too, but Herbert Hoover remained because the lives of hundreds of his mining staff, both foreign and loyal Chinese, were in danger, as well as the property. Lou would not go until he did.

Bert realized that artillery had terminated his employment by the Chinese government. "It is a sorry ending for the program of the Chinese Bureau of Mines," he told his wife, "but if we pull out now many of the Chinese who have been loyal to us foreigners during this trying period will be slain."

The war correspondents stayed on in Tientsin, and Joaquin Miller, the picturesque, bearded poet, was fired with the desire to see Peking. "I want to see the capital city and some of the celebrated places there. I want to go over and look at the Great Wall of China and get farther into this country than a port city."

Lou and Bert warned him that there were Boxer armies

between Tientsin and Peking and foreigners were still under siege in Peking. But Joaquin Miller was undeterred and he hired a ricksha, determined to start out. Lou was convinced that he could not get through alive. To save the situation, she secretly bribed his ricksha boy to desert him en route, and Miller did not get outside of Tientsin.

England, Belgium, France, and Germany all had capital investments in the Chinese Engineering and Mining Company. The Chinese owned the majority interest and managed the business, but a Caucasian technical staff operated the projects. During the Rebellion, in addition to killing hundreds of white people and thousands of their Chinese associates, the Boxers had destroyed much property, which included some holdings of this company which employed Herbert Hoover. After the collapse of the Boxer Rebellion, China agreed to pay reparations to the countries that had suffered at the hands of the Boxers. Also, there were many business relationships to be untangled.

"Chang Yen-mao wants me to buy what is left of the property of the Chinese Engineering and Mining Company for Bewick, Moreing Company of London and reorganize the company into a British corporation," Bert explained to Lou. "He thinks this will save some of the assets."

Mr. Moreing's cable soon arrived, authorizing the reorganization subject to his later approval of the terms. This terminated Herbert Hoover's connection with the Chinese Engineering and Mining Company and shattered his dream of developing the Chinese mines with the financial and technical aid of the British company which had secured his job for him.

In August, Lou Hoover stood in the customs house at Tong Ku with the ousted American Director of Mines for the Chinese empire and comforted him while they waited for the steamer that would take them back to London via the Red Sea and the Mediterranean.

En route, Lou was particularly enthusiastic about the Bay of Naples and began to dream again of a home of her own, maybe overlooking a harbor. She and Bert decided that they needed a place where they could keep some of their possessions, a home base.

From her early camping days away from home, Lou had learned to set up a base for operation. This was never selected hastily. In keeping with her early training, as she discussed with Bert the future prospects for constant travel, London seemed the natural choice, since it was the center of the mining industry development. From this area, Herbert Hoover and other resourceful young Americans with initiative and enterprise would be working to the far corners of the world to develop the commerce that enhanced British colonialism.

When the Hoovers finally arrived in London, Lou found it very exciting to be there. She promptly set out to find a nice apartment which could become the Hoover base of operations, but she dreamed of the time when they would build their own home in California. Her days were filled with looking, but she was homesick and began to realize that this was neither the time nor the place for a permanent home. She returned to the hotel each night with London and New York newspapers under her arm.

Eagerly Lou and Bert read the news from home. They always kept abreast of what was going on in America.

Lou continued to hunt, and finally she found the flat that she wanted, at Hyde Park Gate. Bert heartily agreed with her choice and they moved in. She promptly unpacked some of the things they had brought from China and set about creating their new home. She arranged decorations of flowers and fruits to give it a California atmosphere.

No matter where we go now, she thought, I'll always have this home base. But she still longed for the time when that home base would be in the United States.

decorations of flowers and its to give it a California atmosphere.

No matter where we go now, she thought, I'll always
this longing for a firm foundation for the time
when that home base would be the United States.

IV

CONSTANT TRAVEL

•

1902

THE HOOVERS had been living in their London flat only
a few months when Bert was asked to return to China.
As a newly elected junior partner of the Bewick, Moreing Company, he was commissioned to try to recover
some of the British mining company's property seized
after the Boxer Rebellion.

Lou's zest for adventure had not been dampened by
the excitement and attendant dangers of her firsthand
experiences in China and she was ready to accompany
her husband, even though she had not yet completely
recovered from her dust-storm infection.

She faced the facts squarely as she discussed with Bert
his new partnership responsibilities. Although he would
be returning often to their flat in London, she knew that
he would spend only about a tenth of his time there. The
firm for which he worked had twenty mines in different
parts of the world, and his job was to check operations
in all of them. She must be ready to leave with him on
short notice, be prepared to travel to distant places and
yet maintain a permanent home. They must keep their

London flat at Hyde Park Gate, the couple decided, because it was obvious that Lou could not always accompany Bert on his trips to distant places. When she couldn't go, she would keep the home fires burning for him in London. But nothing could prevent her from going with him now.

When Lou locked the front door of the Hoover flat and put the key away in her purse, she had a secure feeling that no matter how far afield they might travel, they would have this permanent home port in London.

They visited her family in Monterey en route to the Orient. She soon discovered that, after hearing more details of the Hoovers' Tientsin experiences, Charles and Florence Henry were loath to have their daughter return to a country in such turmoil. Her mother in particular feared for Lou's health and safety and urged her not to go into China with Bert. "Think it over well before you decide," she pleaded.

But Lou, who had firmly made up her mind, declared, "Of course I am going. It will be a nice trip to the Orient. I believe Jean would like it, too." She had quickly sensed her sister's hidden dreams.

"Maybe you and Jean could stay in Japan and let me go on into China alone," suggested Bert. "It will be awfully cold there now."

Jean, who was twenty years old, had finished school and was working hard on perfecting her violin technique. She hung on every word as Bert explained his new mission.

"Why not let Jean go with you for the trip to Japan that she is spoiling to take," her father suddenly urged Lou, "and you could stay there with her for a few months."

After much discussion it was agreed that Lou and Jean

should travel to Yokohama with Bert, then let him face the rigors of frozen North China by himself.

The two sisters had a brief, happy time together in Japan, although Lou missed Bert desperately and sent him daily letters. While Lou wrote to her husband Jean kept a lively diary. She described first getting settled in Japan with her sister.

"Lou rented a charming little Japanese house with sliding panels, paper windows, straw mats on the floor and colorful pillows to sit on. Often we put on Japanese kimonos, do up our hair Nippon style, and Yoshi, our Japanese maid, serves us ceremonial tea."

Jean and Lou began to read everything available about the land of their vacation sojourn. At tea they often discussed their findings, as recorded in the diary.

"Lou says Japan has made fantastic strides from a medieval culture to a completely Western pattern, catching up with Europe and outdistancing Russia."

The months in Yokohama were pleasant and restful. Lou Hoover believed in keeping the Sabbath holy and yet she was very indulgent of her sister, as the latter recorded in a diary entry:

"Feb. 3. I forgot it was Sunday and played a game of Bisque with Lou. She thought it was such a good joke that she didn't tell me it was Sunday till we finished."

Jean's diary described many shopping trips. "It snowed this morning but by noon was clear. We went for a walk in the afternoon. Yoshi, Lou, and I visited most interesting toy shops. We had lots of fun and bought a number of funny things. Stopped at a paper store where they make screens. The paper and cloth material for walls is much nicer than the wallpaper is in the foreign stores."

"Visited a porcelain shop we had not seen before. Also

a dry-goods store and bought some pretty material for petticoats.

"We took rickshas and visited a large furniture store. They have beautiful work but much is overly carved for my taste. Then we visited a shoestore and a paper store. Consequently we were too lazy to dress for dinner and had it sent up. Lou is writing to Bert now."

Lou had no difficulty keeping up with her young sister when it came to walking or riding a bicycle.

"Feb. 18. We went on our wheels to see the plum and cherry blossoms. These trees are cultivated for their blossoms only and have no fruit. It was too windy so we turned off and found the prettiest little temple I ever saw. The country was beautiful. We rode fifteen to twenty miles and got home about 5:30.

"We went for quite a long walk and climbed the cliffs above Mississippi Bay. It commanded a most beautiful view. Lou says Naples, Monterey, and this one are all the prettiest ones she has ever seen.

"We rode our wheels out the Tokiedo Road. This is a very old road that connects Tokyo and Kioto the old capital. We went about fifteen miles to Omori which is about halfway between Yokohoma and Tokyo. We came back by train because there was a stiff wind. I woke up next day with an earache."

Jean's violin was still her first love. "I practiced on my violin while Lou and Yoshi went to the doctor. While Lou was out we received a chit asking us to tiffin Sunday. It was a very enjoyable afternoon. The people there were quite musical. They have a Beethoven Society and invited us in to the next meeting.

"I practiced over an hour today. In the evening, twenty of us went into the parlor and had a concert. There was a very good violinist in town for a week, a German from

New York. He really played extremely well." The musical programs were enjoyed by both sisters.

Lou found that her health had greatly improved with the restful months in Japan and she had all of her old energy back. The letters from Bert told of his disappointment with the new management of the Bewick. Moreing Company mines.

Then one day in March Lou dashed into her little Japanese house, her eyes shining with excitement and a letter clutched in her hand.

"Bert is returning and we will be going home soon," she announced. "The letter says that the London office sold out ownership in the coal mines to Belgian and German interests which would not permit Chinese participation." Bert would not remain under these circumstances and so resigned as manager. "We will be off to London soon," she said.

The sisters sailed out of Yokohama in opposite directions, Jean going eastward across the Pacific to San Francisco, while Lou and her husband headed westward to London.

In London, Lou bought all the new furniture that she wanted for the flat at Hyde Park Gate, thinking they would settle down for a while. However, Bert was off to France and Italy very shortly. She decided to stay in the home base through the summer of 1901.

In the fall, Bert brought home the news that he was to inspect the Bewick, Moreing mines in Australia. Lou was delighted because she could accompany him on this trip and because they would go by way of California.

When they arrived in Monterey there was a happy reunion with the Henrys. Then Bert took Lou with him to San Francisco to open a branch office for his company in that city. During their two weeks' stay in San Francisco,

Lou loved to join her husband in the evenings to visit the shops. Once, walking up Vallejo Street, they saw in a second-hand store a steel engraving of Lincoln and his Cabinet by Ritchie. Lou instantly recognized it as a copy of Carpenter's original painting purchased by Mrs. Elizabeth Thompson in 1878 and presented to the nation to hang in the Capitol. Bert liked its authentic detail and its forthright technique. More important, it recorded a great moment in history. They bought the engraving and Lou kept it with them wherever they went to live after that. It was more than a familiar object, it was the symbol of American life, and her husband loved it.

After a pleasant ocean voyage, the Hoovers found their first station in Australia was far from any of the comfortable port cities. They were located at Kalgoorlie, deep in the interior country, which was still inhabited by primitive aborigines. However, in Australia as everywhere else Lou made a delightful home for her husband in one of the American-style company houses built by the Bewick, Moreing Company for its engineers. They arrived in December, summertime Down Under.

Lou knew how disappointed Bert was when he found that while they were in China and London the mining methods and practices of the Sons of Gwalia had retrogressed. As a graduate in geology, Lou took an active interest in the mines. When Bert discussed with her his methods of reforming the organization of the mines to reduce costs and at the same time to increase wages and improve living conditions for the workers, she nodded approvingly and said, "You are a good human engineer, too."

Lou often went with Bert on bicycle trips into the country, where they experienced almost unbelievable heat. Their letters home described this interior of Australia and some of their experiences.

"Bicycles are widely used by the white men. Camels are soft-footed so make a hard pad or track through the softest sand and this makes good bicycle paths in the level country. Long camel rides wrench every muscle in one's body so Bert prefers to go by motor as far as possible, with a bicycle strapped on behind."

When Lou could not go with him he brought her artifacts from his trips and they delved together into the native customs. "From Lake Darlot Bert brought native weapons: two spears, a shield and six boomerangs. He saw some rare emus, three-toed birds about the size of ostriches but having no wings and no feathers, simply hair. The two emu eggs he brought back measure five inches on their major axis."

Lou was a little appalled at some of the native customs and her sympathies were with the women. "There are various dances with peculiar rites. The women dance alone while the men sing. Elaborate ceremonies for food producing center chiefly around fasting to make it rain. The women do all the work. They are not allowed to eat various kinds of meats, the children are denied other kinds, but the men can eat everything. The coast tribes live much better and are physically and mentally superior to those of the interior who are chiefly shepherds."

After several months in the hot interior, Lou welcomed Bert's next assignment to the Broken Hill Mines in the south of Australia, five hundred miles from Adelaide, the port city.

Here the climate was much better and the company houses were landscaped. In the Broken Hill Mines, Bert's job was to develop a new process for extracting zinc from the ore that had been cast aside as useless residue after other metals had been taken out.

"I am enthusiastic about this job," he told Lou, "because it takes the gambling speculation out of mining and makes it a stable business operation."

Because of the success of Bert's new methods at Broken Hill, he was called as consultant to several other mines in Australia. The Hoovers had been away from London for nearly a year when a cable came directing Bert to investigate rumors of an extraordinary lead mine in Burma on his way back to England.

While traveling, the young Hoovers kept abreast of the latest books, ideas, and political trends. "Political currents have a direct bearing on most of the company enterprises," explained Bert, "because the firm of Bewick and Moreing has coal mines in China, Wales, and the Transvaal; a tin mine in Cornwall; gold mines in Australia, New Zealand, Burma, Russia, and Africa; copper mines in Queensland and Canada; a lead-silver mine in Nevada, and a turquoise mine in Egypt."

A few weeks in Burma was a long enough time to convince him that the lead mine was worth developing and he made extensive notes to verify this.

Lou enjoyed the long boat trip back to England with Bert. While strolling the deck on a bright, brisk day, Lou asked, "Now that you have seen most of the mines in the world, wouldn't it be nice to just direct mining operations from the London office? Then we could have a house of our own."

"We will have a house in London," he promised.

One early morning, after a pleasant voyage, the coast of England appeared out of the mist. We will find a house, Lou thought, and Bert will go to his office like other husbands do. I will be a housewife, pay calls, and go to market. We will have children and start to lead a settled, peaceful, ordinary existence.

V

BECOMING A FAMILY

•

1903–1907

IT WAS LATE IN DECEMBER 1902 when Lou returned to
London with her husband from their stay in Australia,
and more briefly in Burma. She was filled with a new enthusiasm for she knew she was to have a baby. Her dream
of settling down in a home of their own seemed about
to be transformed into reality. Bert had been prodigiously
successful in work with his company's mines and would
be assured of a good income.

Children were uppermost in her mind, and a Christmas
visit with the family of the financial manager of the Bewick, Moreing Company made her longing for children
even stronger.

Lou appreciated the atmosphere of the home as she
took off her snowy galoshes and walked over to warm
her hands at the fireplace where a Yule log was burning.
Bert expanded a little as he described Australia, but
gradually he became aware that his host's attention was
obviously on his own thoughts. Meanwhile, Lou and their
hostess watched the four children, happy and excited, as
they opened their gifts around the Christmas tree.

"How wonderful to have children at Christmastime!" she exclaimed.

On the way home she was elated. "It has been a lovely Christmas with the children and next year we will have a child of our own. Life is going to be different now."

The appeal of the children was lingering in Lou's thoughts as she arranged flowers in the Hoover flat the next morning. The telephone rang. It was Bert calling from the office with the tragic revelation that the financial manager had disappeared. "There is no question about it," Bert said flatly, "He left a twenty-page letter of confession."

Lou was stunned to learn that over $700,000 had vanished with their host of the previous evening. He had borrowed the money on the security of the firm and had forged its name to documents. A shocked Lou replied, "It is just unbelievable. What are you going to do about it?"

"The only thing we can do is to see that the company makes good all the losses," he asserted.

Lou was shaken and deeply disappointed. She realized that if Bert carried out the plan he outlined it would mean the loss of their personal fortune and all her plans for a home would be shattered. But her conscience triumphed and she was able to pull herself together by the time Bert arrived home. When she saw him looking a little haggard, all her questions were sympathetic to his attitude.

"Yes, I agree with you," she told him. "The company is morally responsible for money obtained on its credit by one of the partners."

As he visibly relaxed, she calmly assured him, "Of course we will have to uphold the integrity of the firm. It is our obligation."

Her thoughts turned to the future. "You are so good at changing bad mines into good ones," she continued, "that there will be plenty of opportunities. But please promise that you will be back in London before our baby is born."

He gave her an adoring look. "Don't worry, I'll be here," he promised.

"After that," continued Lou, "we will both go with you."

"We'll see," he said enigmatically.

Lou was surprised at the cabled reaction of the absent senior partner and other business associates who argued that the firm could not be held legally liable. In the end, the senior partner returned home from his hunting trip and assumed his share of the losses, leaving about a quarter of a million dollars for the others to pay off.

When the defaulting financial manager was arrested in Canada and sent to prison for ten years, Lou assumed another obligation. Since this man's family had no income, she could not bear to think of what would happen to his wife and the four childen during the prison sentence so she personally gave them an allowance to help support the children until their father's release.

The financial disaster for the great Bewick, Moreing Company was sensational in London and there were many reverberations. Lou stood by her husband steadfastly, discussed points with him, and helped him decide on his own course of action, even though it meant losing the fruits of his past years of hard work in order to keep the company on its feet. Soon they were back in the old groove, working for the Bewick, Moreing Company in far-flung places and proud that it was a firm that had won the respect of the world by meeting all its obligations, both legal and moral.

Bert was working harder than ever, driven by the determination to exonerate his company and by the exhilarating thought that he was soon to be a father and have new responsibilities.

Meanwhile, a bassinet was ready under the Lincoln engraving in the spare bedroom at Hyde Park Gate. During the months of waiting for Bert to return, Lou prepared for the baby.

She had gradually come to the realization that she could have no home, in the physical sense, as long as she was married to Bert. Home for them must be wherever they could be together. Her greatest challenge would be to set up a good home for her family, whether it was in the desert area of Australia or the jungles of Burma. But she was determined that she would go with her husband wherever the mode of travel would permit her to take their baby.

Lou knew that Bert would go to Australia again in the fall. With engineering efficiency, she planned the equipment that would be needed to take proper care of a baby, both on the trip and after they arrived. She found a little folding rubber bathtub which could also serve as the mattress for the baby's bed, which was a large two-handled basket. It was light and could be carried into a train so the baby could always have his own familiar sleeping place and would never have to be put into a strange crib. She prepared two small cabinets, one for the baby's clothes and the other to serve as an icebox.

She engaged a nurse to help her with her preparations, one who agreed to accompany the new baby on his first trip. Bert was home in plenty of time to aid in the final arrangements.

At last the great day came. As Bert ushered the doctor and his two assistants into the house, he asked anxiously, "Are you sure you have everything that will be needed?"

The expectant father paced up and down, his hands

thrust deep into his trousers pockets, feeling he could bear a revolution or a flooded mine much easier than this birth.

Herbert Clark Hoover, Jr., was born on August 4, 1903. His father's apprehension turned into paternal pride as he looked at the wrinkled newcomer who protested so loudly.

"He is going to look like you," declared Lou happily. "Our son is fine and healthy and I am sure he will be a good traveler."

Bert had his namesake registered with the American consul in London at once. "He will be an American citizen," declared his father.

When the baby was five weeks old, his parents and his nurse started for Australia with Herbert, Jr., in the basket.

Even after her baby's arrival, Lou Hoover permitted herself no more wistful wishing for a permanent home. She carried him wherever her husband's work took them. Before little Herbert was a year old, he had been around the world twice. Their home moved with the Hoovers, on passenger liners, trains, stagecoaches, automobiles, and even on horseback. There were always some old familiar possessions along. Lincoln and his Cabinet was the first picture to go up in any new stopping place. Home was where the three were together, surroundings did not matter.

When husband and wife were separated, even though Bert was in some remote part of the world and Lou was in London, the two kept in close touch through letters. He often asked her to mail him information on some technical subject. A dedicated researcher herself, she loved these assignments. She felt that without them she had little enough to do with the things that concerned him.

One time when Bert was in London, Lou made a trip to the British Museum Library to look up some geology material for him and she came across an old copy of *Agricola de re Metallica*. The book, originally published in Latin in 1556, only a hundred years after Gutenberg's Bible, was the standard manual of mining and metallurgy for one hundred and eighty years. The author, Georgius Agricola, was actually George Bauer, a German from Saxony, whose pen name was made up from the literal Latin equivalents of his German name.

That night Lou proudly showed Bert the dusty old copy of *Agricola* which had awed them both in Dr. Branner's laboratory during their college days. She was especially intrigued with the ancient woodcuts used to illustrate the text. "What do you suppose these pictures really mean?" she asked. A translation was already working in her mind. She asked a friend, who knew dealers in old books, to find a copy which she could purchase. One evening she enthusiastically showed her proud new possession to Bert. "It will take some scientific detective work to ferret out the meanings of these old woodcuts, which are such an essential part of the book's effectiveness, but I'd like to try," she began.

The amazingly intricate illustrations were hand-carved in relief on the woodblocks used in the printing. "The trouble is that no mining engineer of today has ever tried to decipher them," she reasoned, showing her husband the quaint prints on the yellowed pages of the old volume. "George Bauer was right there in the mines and when the Latin language didn't have a word for a new process, he invented a word to fit it and made a sketch to clarify the meaning. Translators who don't know mining can't understand him. So all of this knowledge of early mining lies buried because so far no one has been able to dig it out. It's like the low-grade ore you are always working with—the gold is there, but it takes the right combination of knowledge and patience to extract it on a paying basis. Now I'm glad that I took those Latin courses at Stanford."

Bert was soon fired with Lou's enthusiasm and the two spent all the free hours they could manage working together on the translation. Neither could have done the job alone. She borrowed many books and studied out the old Latin forms. Bert experimented in the laboratory to check up on the verity of some of Agricola's statements and straighten out ambiguities. Lou found an early German translation of the book, but it did not turn out to be very helpful. The fascinated pair went to Saxony to study the region and the mines there and also to Friedberg, to the great German school of mines, in search of ancient mining history. Lou kept all their reference books in London but worked at the translation intermittently as they traveled. The translation project extended over a period of five years. It afforded her much pleasure, not only from her husband's enthusiastic company but from her detective work as well.

While on a brief visit to California in June 1905, Lou and Bert left two-year-old Herbert with his aunt Mildred, wife of Theodore Hoover, to get acquainted with his four-year-old cousin Mildred, while they accompanied Theodore on a strenuous pack trip into Yosemite and over Tioga Pass. Small Herbert called his cousin Mindy, and the name stuck.

Not long after that, Bewick, Moreing Company hired Theodore as one of its engineers. Lou looked forward to having relatives living in London. A year later she welcomed the Theodore Hoovers, with Mindy and a new daughter Hulda, when they arrived in England. The Theodore Hoovers lived in London for the next ten years.

Lou and Mildred often took Herbert, with Mindy and Hulda and their English nurses, to Hyde Park or Kensington Gardens to have tea under the trees while the older children sailed toy boats on Round Pond. Dinners were frequently exchanged between the older members of the two families and often they motored into the country, with the children, for picnics.

In the spring of 1907, the Herbert Hoovers were returning from Burma to London by way of California and Lou enjoyed an unhurried visit with her parents and sister Jean. It was with pride and satisfaction that she told them, "Little Herbert has circled the globe three times, and not once has he missed a meal, lost his sleep, or been ill during those long trips by land and sea."

"It doesn't seem possible," commented her mother.

"He is a fine, sturdy boy," contributed Grandpa Charles Henry, "and is going to be much like his father. You should have a girl now, Lou."

Allan Hoover was born in London on July 17, 1907, at the Hyde Park flat. Lou was a happy mother and much interested in the differences in her boys. "This new one is going to look more like my side of the family," she told Bert.

Allan, named for his father's uncle, was registered at the American consulate. When he was five weeks old, the family started off on another trip to Burma. Lou told young Herbert, "It is your little brother who gets to ride in the basket this time."

In anticipation of living in Burma and of much traveling, she made an appointment with a famous child specialist in London. Before her visit, she compiled a list of questions that covered every possible eventuality that she could foresee which might arise during the growing years of her two boys. In a notebook, she recorded the counsel and advice of the doctor as to food, clothing, and medicines for both common and special diseases. With this professional direction, she stocked up provisions of food, drugs, and every possible anticipated article that Herbert and Allan might require while the family was far from civilization. She took a sufficient quantity of hard-to-get articles to last until their return to London. The Hoovers hired a capable English nurse to help take care of the boys.

When they arrived in Burma, they headed for a big silver and lead mine in the north, near the Chinese border. That part of Burma was very mountainous and covered with immense forests. Some of the mountains rose from twelve to nineteen thousand feet. To reach the mine, it was necessary to journey one hundred and thirty miles on the Lashio Railway from Mandalay to Haipaw, capital of a Shan state, where the mine was located. The entire party had to travel sometimes by elephant back and sometimes in sedan chairs as they traversed many miles of jungle.

Lou had looked forward with interest to meeting the local people and she found them "the most truly happy and cheerful race in Asia." The native Sawbwa, or prince, spoke with a perfect Oxford accent as he described his problems to the Hoovers. He had been educated in England and then had returned home to rule his principality, which had been in the family for 1,000 years. He had thousands of relatives and was compelled to marry a wife from each clan. There were now twenty-odd wives and he couldn't afford to keep them all. Besides, he needed a new white elephant. He welcomed anyone who could speak English and told the Hoovers that he hoped he could build roads and schools and towns for his people from the income that he might get from the silver and lead mine.

Very primitive living conditions challenged Lou Hoover to create a safe and comfortable home for the family. There was no possible place at Haipaw, so they took a cottage in Mandalay, at a latitude corresponding to Havana, Cuba, and Canton, China. This ancient city of Mandalay, a one-time capital of Burma, was encompassed by a moat 225 feet wide and had battlement walls 27 feet high. The old palace had become Fort Dufferin after the occupation by the British in 1852.

Lou and their English nurse often took young Herbert to see the houses along the banks of the Irrawaddy River —frail structures of bamboo poles tied together, with matting roofs. Brick houses were to be seen on the main streets, but the bricks were attached to bamboo frames. Pipelines made of split bamboo carried water into the town from the nearby stream.

The Zegyo, one of the finest covered bazaars in the East, was located in the middle of the city. Here were displayed silks, jewels, and sacred images carved in marble and steatite (soapstone) by local artists. Pagodas and monasteries abounded in the region.

In this swampy jungle country, insects were a major health hazard and Lou Hoover feared especially for baby Allan. There were leeches that sucked blood from their victims, small black flies that injected an itch poison, and night-biting buffalo flies so tiny they could hardly be seen that swarmed through the meshes of a mosquito net. The country was full of malaria and one of the problems that Lou faced was to keep the disease-carrying mosquitoes away from the family. In spite of screens and nets and sprays, the mosquitoes won eventually and the whole family contracted malaria. However, their cottage at Mandalay was well screened and drained so, otherwise, the family fared quite well. Here Lou Hoover truly enjoyed her Burmese servants and friends and she had plenty of time to play with her little boys.

In all the primitive mining locations, one of Lou's major concerns, outside of her family, was safety and good housing for the workmen and their families. Often she helped her husband to solve some of the housing problems and work out good sanitation.

It took five years of hard work to transform the Burma mine into a foremost producer. Herbert Hoover did the long-range planning and laid the foundation in about a year of residence and, thereafter, returned at intervals on tours of inspection.

Later, in London, Lou told Mildred Hoover, "Bert had to supervise the building of eighty miles of railroad through the jungle and over two mountain ranges and then he had to create and organize everything at the end of the line. But he loves to make good mines out of bad ones and bring bankrupt mining concerns back to solvency."

Lou and Bert were happy when the Burma tour of duty was ended. En route home, Lou found herself longing for the day when all the Bewick, Moreing Company losses would be covered and the Hoovers could carry out their own family plans.

VI

FREELANCE YEARS

•

1908–1913

LOU WAS GLAD to be home again in her Hyde Park Gate flat early in 1908. At the end of the first month, Bert came home from the office in high spirits.

"We paid off the last of our share of the company indebtedness today, and I then felt free to sell my partnership in Bewick, Moreing to W. J. Loring with the consent of all the other partners, of course," he announced.

"What a wonderful feeling," exulted Lou, "to be out from under that debt."

Over the after-dinner coffee beside the fireplace that evening, Bert told his wife, "Now I will have to rebuild our personal capital to take care of our family. I will start out on my own as an independent consulting mining engineer. My headquarters will have to be London for now."

Many young American engineers flocked to London eager to work for Herbert Hoover in all kinds of mining operations all over the world. When Lou took her boys, now five and one, to see their new cousin Louise, born in London that spring, it was with pride in her heart that she told Mildred Hoover, "Very often mining investors in

75

New York or London put money into the Herbert Hoover Enterprises because they say whether or not his ventures are successful there will be honest administration and complete acceptance of responsibility."

During the next six years, Herbert Hoover became chief consulting engineer and managing director of twenty mining companies. Theodore Hoover left Bewick, Moreing Company to work for his younger brother.

Lou knew that with Bert freelancing in the whole world, there would be no permanent home for them and that her life would continue in the same pattern as during the past six years. First of all, she decided that their London flat was too small for two active boys. The Hoover family needed more space. Her husband agreed that Herbert, Jr., and Allan Henry must have more room to grow up in Western American fashion.

Lou Hoover found a big old place just off Kensington High Street, near Kensington Gardens, with a garden that had real trees in it—and where they could play with the dog young Herbert so longed to have. The roomy, old rusty-red house had an oak-paneled library with a fine big fireplace in it and leaded glass bookcases. The dining room had walnut panels and the living room was decorated in pastel tints.

"The only drawback," Lou told her husband with a twinkle, "is that the seventy-five-year-old lease says that we mustn't let our cows out to wander on High Street nor hang our laundry in sight of the neighbors."

"That part is for you to worry about," he countered.

The house had been made over by Montin Conway, the Alpine author, who called it the "Red House." Lou liked the name and decided to keep it. She immediately picked a spot for the picture of Mr. Lincoln and his Cabinet.

Then she found an Airedale for Herbert, who promptly named the dog Rags.

At the new home, the boys had Javanese seed birds and green parakeets in the house and pigeons and hens in the garden. A big silver Persian cat and a smaller yellow Siamese always showed up at mealtime—and Rags was everywhere.

Every room had bookshelves filled with books on geology, mining, metallurgy, economics, political science, civics, and theories of finance. Then there were many fiction books, several volumes of Sherlock Holmes being among them. Small tables and chairs and all sorts of wheel toys and games were in evidence, with books for the boys also.

Lou enjoyed living in their London headquarters whenever she could not travel with her husband. For eight years the Red House remained the Hoover home between trips to other lands. The whole family enjoyed gathering in the library around the fire. The parents continued to spend happy hours in their joint translation of Agricola. At age six and a half, Herbert, Jr., nicknamed "Pete" by his father, busily scribbled on a tablet announcing, "I'm writing a book, too."

Little Allan, affectionately called "Bub," would climb into his mother's lap demanding, "What does your book say?"

"It's all about mines, darling," Lou very often answered.

Later, Lou Hoover looked back on those years from 1908 to 1914, when she and their sons accompanied Herbert Hoover all over the world, as if through a kaleidoscope. By ship and train and muleback, the family circled the globe, from England to California, to Ceylon, the Malay Peninsula, Japan, Burma, Siberia, and Russia, and back to London again.

A geologist by training and interest and blessed with good health, Lou Hoover experienced with her sons the rough life where railroads were being built and mine shafts sunk. She was not tempted to stay in London for the comforts or regularity of living there, and she never considered dividing the family, unless the education of the boys made this temporarily necessary.

She cleverly planned so that a close, continuous family life could be maintained under the most extraordinary demands of travel and types of residences.

She had to learn how to eliminate the superfluous and to take only the essentials that spell a home. These included treasured toy trains and boats and airplanes only partly finished, baseballs and gloves, some fondly familiar pieces of furniture, the steel engraving of Mr. Lincoln, and almost always, Rags. It mattered little to the boys if they looked out on unknown streets and heard alien tongues around them because inside each strange house their mother had established a familiar home. The boys had a round-the-world education, their geography and history became living realities, naturally absorbed as they met all manner and races of people. Summers were often spent in London or visiting Bert, when that was possible.

When they were in the Red House, Lou and Mildred often took their children to the London Zoological Gardens where Herbert and Mindy especially enjoyed the animals, while Allan and Louise preferred to play on the lawn. As opportunity permitted, the two Hoover families visited Westminster Abbey, the Tower of London, the Wallace Art Collections, and other museums and art galleries.

The Herbert Hoovers enjoyed doing things as a family. Whenever the busy father's schedule permitted, he and Lou took Herbert and Allan to the cathedrals, museums, and restaurants in other parts of England, France, Germany, and Italy. These devoted parents wanted their boys to get a sense of the art, history, literature, and cultural institutions shared in common by the United States and Europe.

In London, Lou let the boys see the depressed standards of living of homeless derelicts who slept in the parks while upper-class people across the street dwelt in luxury. The boys became attached to their own household servants and asked their parents many questions about rich and poor people in British society.

Socially, Lou Hoover sensed an attitude of complete condescension toward Americans and she heard cynical remarks about American women who bought titles. Sometimes she allowed the children to watch weddings at the church on a nearby corner. One day she overheard Herbert explaining to his cousin Mindy, "If the red carpet goes down and the awning goes up, it will cost five shillings extra."

"How much does that make the wedding cost?" asked Mindy.

"Well, you have to count the bridesmaids and listen to know how many peals of the bells there are before you know the whole cost," he answered.

One summer weekend the two Hoover families made a trip to Whit Church, in Hampshire, to hunt for records of Mildred's ancestors. They found the records of the ancestors of the Brooke family in the rectory of the church. Bert looked on with amused tolerance while Lou and Mildred made rubbings of the brass inscription about the father of the Maryland colonist, and took many pictures of the marble statue in the rectory.

As important as this exposure to Europe was, Lou and Bert decided that their boys should have an American education, so the kaleidoscopic view of these years showed them in Palo Alto during the school terms.

The Hoovers rented a cottage on the Stanford campus and Herbert, Jr., and Allan attended the Campus School, along with Mindy Louise and Hulda, their cousins.

Herbert Hoover, who returned to Palo Alto at intervals, agreed with his wife that California should be their permanent residence. They bought property on San Juan Hill, overlooking the Stanford campus. "Here is where we will build our own home someday!" exulted Lou.

During these years, Lou's sons gave her ever-increasing pleasure. When active Allan showed a special ability for taking apart his mechanical toys, methodical Herbert always tried to reassemble them. Their mother encouraged their curiosity by helping them to explore the interest of the moment to their hearts' content. On one long train trip from New York to San Francisco, Lou gave the boys a small alarm clock and a screw driver and they amused themselves dismembering the clock and trying to get all the pieces together again—and working!

In 1911, the entire Hoover family spent several months at Stanford because Herbert was asked by the university to give lectures on the principles of mining.

While Lou enjoyed living on the campus of her Alma Mater, she kept dreaming about the home the family would build there someday.

The boys found plenty of companions to help them explore the surrounding hills, and Lou had many devoted friends on the campus who were willing to look after the boys when she had opportunities to make short trips with her husband.

They were all pleased when Theodore Hoover bought the Rancho del Oso, in the Santa Cruz Mountains, and built a weekend retreat house.

Lou frequently took advantage of their nearness to visit her parents in Monterey. On many weekends the neighbors saw her bundle Herbert and Allan—and usually Rags—into her small open car, which she drove herself, and head for her beloved mountains and sea at Monterey.

Determined that her sons should come to know some of her own free childhood experiences out-of-doors, she loved to share bird and plant and insect mysteries with them, as well as to direct their rock collections. At one time, the Hoover household included two dogs, four turtles, and a large family of frogs which the boys wanted to take down to show to their grandparents. Picnics and camping topped the list of favored family activities, and whenever their father was with them there was always some engineering feat to be performed that would require ingenuity and involve the boys, from building a tree house at the top of a tree that was difficult to climb, to damming up a small stream or building a bridge across it or digging a tunnel.

Even though the family could afford more, the boys' allowances for pocket money were small. "We will keep your spending money small enough for you to appreciate values and also remove the temptation of squandering," explained their mother, "and we think that this will help you to build self-discipline."

When Herbert Hoover's lectures at Stanford were finished, he was asked to repeat them at Columbia University in New York City. Lou helped him put the material into textbook form. They both felt strongly the necessity of including a chapter devoted to the character training and obligations of students who enter the profession of mining engineering. The last chapter urged the highest professional ethics and a genuinely benevolent attitude toward mankind.

As soon as the Columbia lectures were finished, Herbert, Sr., was off to Europe again, headed for Russia. Lou stayed on in New York for several weeks to see *Principles of Mining* through the press while the boys finished school in Palo Alto. As soon as school was out that spring, Lou took the boys back to London, where their father could join them quite often.

The Red House remained their home in London, a place of sunshine, firelight, of children and dogs. Here Lou skillfully handled all sorts of social situations, from children's parties to entertaining celebrities. She was concerned that the place should be homelike as well as beautiful, and she wanted her boys to develop a world point of view as they met the steady stream of assorted visitors to their home. These included their father's friends and business associates, American engineers back from building bridges in Afghanistan or prospecting in Borneo, miners from Nome or the Klondike, Chinese mandarins or businessmen, Stanford professors on research travels, and newspaper correspondents. These world travelers often talked freely about what they had seen of the troubled state of affairs in Europe.

In 1912, Dr. David Starr Jordan, president of Stanford University, returning from peace conferences at the Hague, stopped to visit at the Red House. He talked of the new Hague, of the growth of international understanding, of the hope that through this the world would be led to an era of peace that would make war impossible.

Lou saw her Quaker husband's enthusiasm mounting as Dr. Jordan painted a new society functioning for the welfare of human beings, but Bert's only comment was, "The world was never so full of peace talk—nor so busy putting on its side arms."

All three were tremendously interested in the news that

China had become a republic that year. And all three were pleased that Bert had been elected to the board of trustees at Stanford.

That fall, Lou returned to Palo Alto to put the boys in school and to add some finishing touches to the Agricola manuscript which had been the source of so much interest and pleasure for her and her husband during their spare time in far places.

Their English translation of *Agricola de re Metallica*[1] was published in 1912, in a private edition of 640 copies, bound in white vellum, complete with scrupulously exact reproduction of the old woodcuts which had so intrigued Lou at the outset. The book was dedicated to Dr. John Caspar Branner, their first professor of geology, and carried the names of Herbert and Lou Hoover as joint authors. The best description of the content of the volume appears on the title page: "A Translation from the Latin Edition of 1556, with a Biographical Introduction, Annotations and Appendices upon the Development of Mining Methods, Metallurgical Processes, Geology, Minerology and Mining Law from the Earliest Times to the Sixteenth Century."

Both of the authors were given honorary citations from Stanford in recognition of their joint achievement.

Lou was always happy at Stanford. She began sketching her ideas for the permanent home they planned to build on San Juan Hill while the boys were busy at school.

Herbert and Allan came to look forward to visiting their father at the end of each school year, no matter where he might be stationed.

"Your father is at Kyshtim in the Ural Mountains in Russia," Mrs. Hoover told her sons in the spring of 1913,

[1] This book is on display at the Hoover Institution, Stanford University.

"and there is no very good place to live, but we will go to see him for a few weeks."

The mining center of Kyshtim was located on a run-down old estate half as big as Belgium, which belonged to the Romanoff family. In this remote, inaccessible community, the Hoovers were associated with 170,000 people who were dependent on the copper and iron mines for a living. As Lou saw it, there were complicated layers of people involved, with the Russian noble families at the top, priests and overseers in between, and 100,000 peasants at the bottom.

Herbert Hoover's company built a new town for workers with warm log houses, schools, churches, theaters, and a hospital, and they also established technical schools to train mechanics and paid higher than the local wages to get the best workers.

"The Russian engineers get along exceptionally well with the Americans and there is a notable lack of any Oriental squeeze or patronage," Bert told Lou.

"The wives and families of the engineers and miners are happy in their new homes," she replied.

Under Hoover's management, the mines began to pay and living conditions for the workers were greatly improved so that a prosperous and happy community was built up.

Later that summer of 1913, after their visit to Russia, Lou stood in the garden of the Red House, contentedly watching her sons play croquet. They are growing rapidly, she thought, and have seen a good deal of their father in spite of circumstances. And it's a peaceful world.

But events were conspiring to spoil her peace, as tensions built up in Europe.

Lou listened to much discussion of Germany's lust for power as travelers passed through her home. She knew that Kaiser Wilhelm, who always wore military uniforms with capes, to cover his withered left arm, claimed God as his Divine Ally when he invaded Poland. She heard that the Kaiser's son, the Crown Prince, had been nurtured on this German propaganda and believed that there would be a German victory over all of mankind.

She wondered how war could be avoided in Europe, and hoped that American leaders could help preserve peace, since Philosophy Professor Woodrow Wilson was in the White House. We know Wilson is a peace-loving man, she thought, and perhaps he can help work out a plan to adjust national disputes.

Although she often longed to settle down in California, Lou Hoover pointed out to a visitor from Stanford, "Bert can't withdraw completely from the big mines like the one in Russia without endangering other people's investments. And my business is to be his partner and give him aid and comfort in all his life work."

"Bert is completely happy," she continued, "when his mines are creating productive enterprises, giving jobs to men and women, fighting against whims of nature and inefficient methods."

That fall, Lou told her sons, "The Czar has asked for your father again, this time in Siberia, because he was so successful in the modernization of the Kyshtim estate."

Bert went alone to Siberia, but he wrote illuminating details about his experiences to his wife. The Siberian mines were the so-called "convict mines" where a great many political prisoners had been condemned to hard labor. The Irtish Mines produced zinc, iron, lead, copper, and coal, but the properties were located near the Manchurian border in the bleak, inaccessible Siberian steppes.

Lou reported to one of their engineer friends, "Bert is building 350 miles of railway to make the mines accessible to the Irtish River. Also, he is building boats to transport ore and coal by river to the seaport. He thinks there is tremendous potential in the mines and has invested large amounts of English and Canadian capital as well as a lot of our own money in the building up of this great establishment."

When beginnings of World War I broke out in Europe, the Bolsheviki revolutionists took over the whole Siberian project and Herbert Hoover was evacuated to Vladivostok, along with sixty American engineers, plus their wives and children.

Bert headed at once for California, where he arrived just before the Christmas holidays, a disappointed and unhappy man. Lou saw Bert's dream of developing successful mines crumble again, just as he was on the threshold of achieving a great personal fortune.

VII

WORLD WAR I AND
BELGIAN RELIEF

•

1914–1916

EARLY IN MARCH 1914, Lou took her boys out of school so
that they could accompany her and their father to Europe.
Bert had been asked by the sponsors of the Panama
Pacific International Exposition, scheduled for San Francisco, to try to enlist the participation of European countries in the exhibits.

En route to Europe, the family stopped in New York to
attend a dinner given in honor of Lou and Herbert
Hoover at the Biltmore Hotel, on March 9 by the Mining
and Metallurgical Society of America. Lou's pulse speeded
up as a gold medal was presented jointly to her and her
husband for translating *Agricola*. She felt very proud
when they were cited for making available for the first
time this ancient and basic authority on metallurgy and
mining.

The Hoover family was happy to be back in the Red
House in London, together. After discussing the matter
with Bert, Lou planned that she and the boys, then ten
and six years old, should stay in London until their father's
birthday, August 10. Bert arranged a return passage for

them on the *Lusitania,* around the middle of August—a voyage which was later canceled because of the war situation.

When on June 28 the Archduke of Austria and his wife were shot by Serbian conspirators, Lou realized that this was more than just a crime committed in a remote Balkan village. She feared that the murder of Francis Ferdinand might precipitate a war because of the mass hatreds in the various European countries which she had seen. She and Bert pondered the world situation as they knew it in that summer of 1914, but even they could not foresee that this Balkan murder would launch the overwhelming cataclysm of the European conflagration that spread over the next four years.

"Will there be a war over this murder?" Lou asked her husband.

"The murder of the Grand Duke would not in itself cause war," he replied, "but it might be the trigger to set off an explosion. You and I have traveled enough to see some of the underlying causes of national animosities which could flare into a war. There is greed for nationalism and also for prestige. There are expanding ambitions and economic rivalries for spheres of influence and, of course, worst of all, there is militarism."

"I guess you think war is inevitable." She sighed.

Lou had planned that the weekend of August 1 was to be spent with their long-time friends, the Edgar Rickards, at their summer cottage in Westgate. She and Bert drove with the boys on a sunshiny Saturday afternoon. The two families expected to have an advance joint celebration of the birthdays of Herbert, Sr., and Jr., and the boys were hiding the gifts for their father in a covered basket.

That was the day Germany declared war on France! The next day, Germany stated her intention to violate the neutrality of Belgium. The birthday party was postponed indefinitely.

Sunday morning, the two families at Westgate went to the Village Inn for lunch and discussed the tense situation. They bought extra tins of gasoline for the drive back to London.

The German army invaded Belgium. Reports began crossing the Channel that the soldiers had shot down civilians and carried on extensive looting and wanton destruction of towns. On August 4, England declared war on Germany.

Lou read the news in shocked dismay, although for weeks she and Bert had been uneasily aware of the national tensions developing as the war cauldron began to boil. President Woodrow Wilson proclaimed the neutrality of the United States, also on August 4, and the next day he offered to go to the Hague to mediate the war disputes. The stunned Western world thought civilization was pulled up by its roots. Lou sensed an apprehensive atmosphere in England as the newspapers wrote of the tragic catastrophe. People who had lived secure lives in a safe and tranquil world failed to comprehend the full meaning of the reports. Shopkeepers were dazed but put up signs, "Business as Usual."

Lou Hoover was uniquely in a position to do a valuable service in this great emergency because she had served as president of the American Women's Club in London and had given appreciated leadership to many of their activities.

Her life for the next few weeks is best described in her own words, in a letter to her parents written from the Red House and mailed from London August 22, 1914.[1]

[1] This letter is now in possession of Mrs. Hoover's niece, Mrs. Delano Large.

Since August fifth we have been *working*. Got back from the country the night of the 3rd. We celebrated Herbert's birthday the 4th at home. About 2:30 Bert telephoned to ask me for 100 pounds in money which I happened to have in the house, and said if I wanted to see an interesting sight to come down. Early in the day a few people whom Bert knew had turned up at his office for money. And later the consul, quite a new man, had telephoned to ask Bert's advice and assistance because of the hundreds arriving there. So Bert took what money he could gather up about the office and my hundred pounds and some he could get from his friends and went over to the consulate and began lending out money (of course without interest) in small amounts to American tourists to live on a few days. He took care of over 300 that day.

Many of Lou's friends were among the 70,000 Americans traveling in Europe that summer who found themselves penniless and helpless because of the sudden disrupting turn of events.

The shops were open but would take only cash and small checks of their own customers. The banks were all shut and most of the large and influential places were too.

No one would take continental paper money, which most of them had, nor letters of credit nor continental nor American bank checks or drafts, nor American Express and similar checks nor even American paper money! Of course any kind of gold was taken at its weight. But there wasn't much of that. Most of the shops refused to take even English paper money if they had to make change in return! And of course there were all sorts of rumors as to boats being taken off and no possibility of getting home and nearly everybody was rather panicky. A tourist committee of some bankers and other active men had been formed the day before to see about getting transports from home, or doing something else to get themselves (and as many others as possible) home. They had met at the Savoy—a big hotel we knew very well. And Bert had been in to see them, and said there were lots of ladies arriving there for aid and sympathy.

Lou's immediate natural reaction was to respond to this emergency, to help the stranded women and children.

So I went down to the hotel before ten o'clock, saw the perfect pandemonium there, called half a dozen women whom I knew would keep their heads and could work, and offered to look after the women and children who had no men with them. They made me the only woman member of the big men's committee, and my women made me chairman of our women's committee and since that I have worked day and night, and certainly left the boys to Amy! But none of us could think of just the right other person to do it instead of me. We made all sorts of arrangements whereby people could get money on their credits.

Bert established a wonderful telegraphic money order system that started work immediately and produced the money in 24 or 48 hours—although the regular telegraph systems have not yet caught up with their work. When there was no other way of getting money we lent it to them. We got them boarding places, clothes (lots of them had lost even their suitcases), found their relatives for them and made arrangements for shipping them home when the boats began to move again.

Nearly 40,000 of them have been sent home in the three weeks and it is estimated there are between 10,000 and 20,000 still here with a few hundred arriving from the continent every day. Well, altogether it has made a lot more work than it sounds in this letter.

We have not even thought when we should start home. Of course both the boats we had passage on have been taken off.

Lou met daily at the Savoy Hotel with the stranded American women, taking over the job of caring for all the unaccompanied women and children, frightened and bewildered by the calamity of sudden war. While transportation was being commandeered for them in American and neutral ships, Lou arranged lodgings for them in London. She also organized friendly tours to see the London sights, cathedral towns, and Shakespeare country, in order to fill their time and try to distract them, as more and more drifted in from the continent with tales of horror.

She enlisted the aid of the American Women's Club to provide used clothing for some of the more destitute travelers. She helped them borrow the money they needed to live on, while their passage across the Atlantic was paid for by the United States government, after telegraphic identification. More than 90 per cent of those who received aid in London returned the money expended on them after they returned home.

"Why do all those people need money?" inquired Herbert of his mother. "Didn't they bring any with them?"

"Most of them brought letters of credit," she explained, "and those letters depend upon people trusting each other's promise to pay. When there is war, people don't trust each other."

Finally, after booking and canceling passage home on five different ships, Lou and her boys boarded the Cunard liner, again the *Lusitania,* on October 3, intent upon getting Herbert and Allan back to school in Palo Alto.

"I'm sorry not to be going with you," Bert said to Lou, "but it looks as if my responsibilities will be in Europe just now."

"Yes," replied Lou, "I understand."

Herbert had dreaded the trip, fearing seasickness, to

which he was prone, but was able to send his father a triumphant message from New York on October 9 that on board ship he had not missed a meal and had held down seven cream puffs in one day!

When the three Hoovers arrived in Palo Alto, Lou engaged a housekeeper, organized her household in the cottage on the campus, and helped Herbert and Allan get settled into their programs at the Campus School. Finally, she felt the boys would be safe and secure under the supervision of their aunt Mildred, who lived nearby, and close friends on the faculty at Stanford, if she left them for short intervals.

She was greatly perturbed by conditions among the conquered civilians which she had seen developing in Europe and felt that the American people should know more about the situation. Her sympathy went out especially to the women and children of Belgium and their plight galvanized her into action.

Lou Hoover naturally shrank from public speaking. "I'm really scared to death," she told her sister Jean. But, once convinced that it was her duty as well as her privilege to tell American women what she had learned while in Europe, she accepted many speaking engagements on behalf of the stricken Belgians. With the greatness of simplicity, she pictured the terrible conditions in Europe in a way that brought instant response.

> "In Belgium they have no homes, no food, in seven provinces out of nine the Belgians have nothing. It is not easy for comfortable folk to realize this, to grasp what it means. Yesterday to have had a house to live in, today to have nothing but the clothes on your back, hurrying away from your village on fire. Old men, women, and children—mothers with babes at the breast—they hurry and hurry—they stumble and fall.

"In the red track of war, follows famine and bitter want. Will you give whatever you can? The twin sisters of sympathy and charity have never wandered very far from the State of Liberty."

She spoke in San Francisco on October 23, 1914, urging American relief to Belgium, and made numerous other appearances in the area, to expedite the work of sending supplies and money.

She was instrumental in raising $100,000 in the San Francisco Bay region alone. She showed unusual ability to cut red tape and persuaded the Rockefeller Foundation to provide free shipping of all the American Relief food and clothes to Belgium.

From San Francisco, she moved south to Los Angeles. Having been commissioned by King Albert of Belgium to aid the movement in America for the relief of suffering among the noncombatants in Belgium, she addressed a mass meeting in Los Angeles on November 14. When the mayor introduced her he said:

"Mrs. Hoover has lived in Belgium and knows the character of the Belgian peasantry. In her own home in London today are three Belgian women with their children, whose husbands are at the front, perhaps never to return. These are but the type of many thousands being cared for in English homes."

Lou was not a professional speaker but she spoke from experience and from her heart.

"These people love their homes. They love Belgian soil with the passionate love of people who have fought for that soil, and whose fathers and grandfathers have fought for that same soil. They all said that if Belgium fell permanently into the hands of Germany the whole nation would come to America.

"Their history has been so turbulent that as a class they have had little time to do anything more than exist. Thrift they have developed and they work their farms busily and well. They are people of great strength of character."

In the Los Angeles area, Lou Hoover met many of her old friends who knew her as Lou Henry of Whittier and Monterey. They admired her achievements and quickly acknowledged her as among the finest Americans of those troubled times.

Miss Edith Jordan, head of the history department of the Polytechnic High School in Los Angeles, and daughter of David Starr Jordan, Stanford's first president, said of her, "She is the most capable woman alive."

With all this public acclaim and, no matter how demanding the war project, Lou Hoover's first concern continued to be her desire to fulfill adequately her responsibilities as wife and mother, so she hurried back to Palo Alto to plan for the boys' Thanksgiving holiday.

She spoke at the Stanford University home of John C. Branner, Stanford's second president, on the subject of Belgian relief work. She told how Belgium was doomed with 7 million peaceful, hard-working citizens caught between armies. Many Belgians were killed by the German soldiers driving through their country to reach France, while many others were being starved by the iron ring of the British blockade of their ports. She explained that Germany would allow America to send food to Belgium through Holland with the Allies' consent, provided that the work was done by Americans under German surveillance. Finally, she told how her husband had been asked by the American Friends Service Committee and the Red

Cross to tackle this tremendous humanitarian task when a whole nation of men, women, and children was starving.

"I'm telling you this," she said, "because you are our friends and neighbors, and you know how proud I am of Bert."

The university community was a responsive audience and soon the Stanford faculty agreed to duplicate any sum raised by the students for this purpose. People were so moved by Lou's talks that the combined committees from San Francisco and Los Angeles were able to secure a shipload of food and sent it through the Panama Canal to Belgium.

Lou's thoughts were constantly with Bert, who remained in Europe, and in early December she returned to London to join him. That Lou's husband truly appreciated her is proved in his *Memoirs*:

> She intrepidly defied the dangers of the North Sea and went with me on my second journey to Brussels where we arrived just before Christmas. She visited every sort of relief activity. On Christmas Day she attended the special service at the shrine of all Belgians, the Cathedral of St. Gudule. The hundreds of women in the deepest of mourning, the emotional response of the great audience to the moving prayers of the priest for safety of their loved ones and for delivery from their oppressions left her greatly affected by the spiritual tragedy which had overwhelmed the Belgian people. Her question was, "Do these Germans think they can hold a people whose very souls revolt?"

During the war, Lou quietly accepted the fact that her family could not be together, mainly since Herbert and Allan stayed in Palo Alto to attend school. She was with Bert enough to know about his tremendous undertaking and thoroughly agreed with his plans to finance his part of the Belgian relief operation personally. He was completely immersed in a project of public service, putting aside his own business and self-interests. He had built up a small private fortune from his mining, so asked for and received no salary, and paid all his own expenses, as he traveled constantly from the Belgian Relief headquarters in London to Holland, Belgium, Germany, Switzerland, and France. He brought the great asset of his engineering efficiency to the money raising, food buying, and securing of the transportation necessary for the daily feeding of 10 million imprisoned people in occupied Belgium and France.

Lou commuted between her husband and her sons during the years 1915 and 1916. Twice before America's entrance into the war, she brought the boys to the Red House to stay awhile with their father.

She read about the long Battle of the Marne that extended through the fall and winter of 1914–1915, as the English and French armies drove the Germans back to the Aisne River, where the Allies dug trenches extending from Nieuport on the English Channel to the Swiss frontier. War news was anxiously scanned in London as the civilians valiantly tried to do their part to aid the victims of the fighting abroad as well as at home.

Lou, who was still president of the American Women's Club in London, was a recognized leader in this effort. From the club membership there evolved, during those first hectic days of helping stranded Americans at the Savoy Hotel, the American Women's War Relief Committee. Other able and hard-working recruits augmented the committee's membership. Many of the members were American women married to prominent Britishers. All were eager to support, with both their means and their intelligence, the various relief projects undertaken.

From her banker father, Lou Henry Hoover had learned to keep meticulous accounts, so it was natural that she would be asked to use this ability in her war work. Her particular job was that of accounting agent, and she had scrupulous records kept of all expenditures of the American Women's War Relief funds, which started one of the greatest relief campaigns the world has ever known.

Mrs. Hoover also gave practical, personal help as chairman of a committee which established canteens in all the leading railway stations in London. As she stood one cold day at the Paddington Station, handing out sandwiches, coffee, and other quick refreshments to servicemen in uniform, she explained to an American visitor, "This is a great boon to thousands of soldiers who pass through London daily, because many of them are without sufficient money to buy food. It was our American clubwomen working in the railway stations, looking after stranded American and Belgian refugees, who learned of the great need for canteens where soldiers can be provided promptly with nourishing food at no cost."

Never content with what had already been accomplished, Lou was always expanding the program. In addition to the canteens, the Women's Committee carried out three major projects:

They maintained the American Women's War Hospital; operated a fleet of six Red Cross motor ambulances; and carried out a scheme of economic relief for British women out of work.

Lou seemed indomitable even when challenged by all sorts of seemingly impossible situations. As chairman of a committee to find a house large enough to serve as a hospital, she inspired Mr. E. Paris Singer to offer his magnificent mansion, Oldway House, at Paignton, near the famous watering place, Torquay, on the Devonshire coast.

Mr. Singer, who had amassed a fortune in America through his sewing machines, donated $25,000 toward the cost of equipment and personally supervised the conversion of his house into a hospital.

Lou constantly kept an eye to the future. The expansion of the hospital was a matter of improvising. Years of travel had given Lou Hoover an uncanny understanding of soldiers' needs so she could anticipate what they would want. She examined the fourteen wards, accommodating 200 patients, and saw the possibility of adding another 60 to 70 beds should the need arise.

"The conservatory can be converted into a laboratory," she said, "and we will ask the American Red Cross to send a pathologist to do the work." The largest ward was originally a gymnasium, while another had been an indoor riding ring. The hospital was effectively staffed by British and American doctors and nurses. Dr. Ernest Lane was the chief medical officer and Miss Gertrude Fletcher, the matron, who had gained her experience in war hospital management during the South African campaign, was in charge of the nurses.

Situated on a hill in a beautiful grove of trees, no other hospital had better natural surroundings for its patients. In the spring of 1915, on a money-raising tour of America, Lou Hoover described the place:

"Often the wounded boys arrive after dark and townspeople gather to lend a hand if possible. One mother discovered her own son among the wounded, and she had no previous knowledge of it but recognized him as he was being taken from the train. Every patient has but one thought when he gets to the hospital and that is the long-looked-for bath and then the mug of hot soup. Some of the men have not had their clothes off in weeks, but once they are installed between clean white sheets they are oblivious to all the noise about them. In the morning they enjoy the music of donated records and the chance to smoke a cigarette.

"A great feature of this work is that total hospital patient expenses are borne by the American Women's War Relief Fund and no allowance of any kind is taken from the government.

"Red Cross ambulances operated by the Women's Committee are used as needed and contribute to proper care of the wounded."

Back in London, Lou Hoover was deeply concerned when she realized that unemployment had hit the women most and that there was much distress among the poor women and girls of London who had lost their livelihood as a result of the wartime closing of factories. Many women were actually starving. In her own mind Lou thought, it is an impossible task, but we must try. She made a survey to find the greatest consumer need and started a knitting factory in an old pub and later moved it to the headquarters of the YWCA on Barnsbury Street. A second workroom for sewing was started at Woolwich and another knitting factory in Islington, one of the poorest and most congested districts. A good midday meal of meat, vegetable, and pudding was provided for four cents a head through help from the National Food Fund.

Always diplomatic, Lou arranged in advance that the rate of pay in the workrooms was to be approved by the trade unions and none of the materials turned out was sold on the open market to interfere with existing trades. Gloves and socks from the new knitting factories were sent to the boys on the English flagship, *The Iron Duke*, and to other ships and to the combat troops.

The Washington *Post*, during February 1915, put into words a description of Lou Hoover's strong perseverance in a series of articles describing her part in the American Women's War Relief program:

> Mrs. Hoover has a real Yankee temperament and personality and will stand no nonsense. It was she who got several Americans out of Austria and Germany at the beginning of the war. When she takes a thing in hand it is as good as done.

Even though deeply engrossed in her war-relief work, Lou left London on May 10, 1915, to look after her boys, planning to make some more appeals for money while she was in the United States. She just missed getting a booking on the *Lusitania,* which was sunk by a German submarine off Kinsdale Head, Ireland, on May 7, 1915, with the drowning of 1,198 persons, among them 114 Americans.

Safely at home in the States again, Lou always knew the right things to talk about and her speeches carried real messages. She filled many speaking engagements and gave firsthand accounts of life in Europe. She explained that credit had disappeared, stocks and certificates had become only pieces of paper, and even currency had lost its value, as the whole machinery of life was jolted off its base.

She read the war news with a troubled mind, as German military power defeated the Russian forces, then overran Poland and penetrated deeply into Russia. She realized that the failure of Allied military operations in 1915 resulted in very little change on the Western Front and the Germans were not dislodged from their trenches. Therefore, the probability was that the war would be prolonged and that Bert would still be needed in Europe. She must figure a way to keep her family together. During the summer months to come, her boys must have an out-of-doors vacation and perhaps by fall Bert's plans would be crystallized. In spite of her dedication to her work for Belgian relief, her boys always came first.

When school was out in Palo Alto, Lou and the boys planned a number of camping trips for the summer. Herbert and Allan were twelve and eight now, old enough to love Yosemite and the High Sierra.

"I wish Dad could go with us, too," said Herbert.

"Of course, dear, we all wish that as much as you do. But since that is impossible, let's decide what to take with us."

"Rags!" exclaimed Herbert, gathering up the Airedale terrier, his boon companion. Cats, especially Persian or Siamese, were popular pets in the Hoover household, but Rags was the only pet sure to be taken along on trips. Camping always remained the first choice of the whole family for recreation and the boys knew that their mother would join them enthusiastically in hunting, fishing, trapping, and cooking and sleeping out-of-doors.

Unsuspected by them, however, Lou Hoover's mind was in great turmoil as she studied the stars at night and followed the mountain trails by day. She had come to feel that, crisis or no crisis, her family should no longer be separated, so by the end of the summer she had decided not to leave the boys behind in California when she returned to London. In October, the family joined Herbert Hoover in New York, where he had come in connection with his relief work, and the whole family sailed for London on November 9, 1915.

So that the family could be together as much as possible, the boys were enrolled in a small private school near the Red House, which continued to be the center for Belgian Relief activities.

Life in the Red House was exciting in 1915–1916 and provided plenty of dramatic situations, according to Mr. Hoover's *Memoirs:* [2]

In the private school the boys quickly acquired the Oxford accent in full.

The Germans had begun to drop bombs on London from zeppelins. One night during a raid, a bomb dropped nearby with a great explosion. Mrs. H. ran to the boys' room to gather them up, intending to go to the basement, but their beds were empty. We furiously searched the house from attic to basement, but no boys. It then occurred to me that they sometimes climbed up a ladder thru a trap door from the attic onto the roof. Pushing up the trap door, we found them calmly observing the streaming searchlights and the fighting planes. We decided to join them and behold we witnessed a zeppelin brought down in flames north of London. We mentally marked the direction and as soon as it was daylight we got out the car and went in search of the wreck. With the help of a friendly policeman, both boys came home with treasured parts of the zeppelin which clashed with our other household gods for years.

For reasons like this, plus the fact that I had to be on the continent about two-thirds of my time and also that the boys should wear off the Oxford accent and soak in the American way of life, Mrs. H. decided to return with them to California. When she left the Red House in March 1917 for the railway station, we remarked with some sadness that it was probably the last we would see it—and it was. The house with its quaint garden in the middle of a great city was a place of many affections, many happy recollections, and of many stimulating discussions.

After a year and a half in London, Lou Hoover and her sons returned to a rented house on the Stanford campus

[2] Quoted with permission.

late in March, with plans to remain there until the war was over and the father of the family could join them to help make it their permanent home.

How long will it be, Lou wondered, until America is obliged to enter the war. The answer was very shortly forthcoming, since the United States had broken off diplomatic relations with Germany in February and finally, on April 6, declared war on Germany.

Because of her firsthand information, Lou was asked on April 13 to talk to the Stanford faculty and student body about Germany's unrestricted submarine warfare, which precipitated the declaration of war by the United States. When she returned to the Hoover cottage after this speech, Lou went out into her garden. As she walked among the flowers she thought, I'm glad our country has finally entered the war because it seems inevitable and justified, and it probably means that Bert will come home.

After war was declared, President Woodrow Wilson almost immediately asked Herbert Hoover to return to the United States to be the Food Administrator. The loyal American humanitarian accepted this appointment without salary and with the stipulation that he could continue to conduct the Belgian Relief, with the Dutch and Spanish governments distributing the food to Belgium.

His brother Theodore had completed settling the Herbert Hoover business interests in London and had returned to the United States with his family in November 1916.

VIII

FOOD ADMINISTRATION AND

RELIEF YEARS

•

1917–1920

ON A WARM DAY in May 1917, Lou stood on the dock in New York, where she had stood so many times before, and watched the arrival of the big ship that was bringing her husband home. Soon he was by her side. He held her hands and asked, "How are things going, dear?"

"Pretty well," she answered, "but it will be much better now that you are here. Do you realize that you have been with our boys for a total of only about six months in the last three years?"

The Hoovers went directly to Washington and rented a small house on Sixteenth Street for the summer. It was the only place they could find available in the crowded capital.

After only a few weeks, Lou traveled to California to get the boys, whose school session was over. In spite of the war, in spite of the long hours of work required of Herbert Hoover, in spite of the Washington heat, it was a happy summer for the reunited family.

Every Sunday, Lou planned picnics for them in the rolling hills of Virginia. Usually they were joined by the

Edgar Rickards and other Food Administration families. Young Herbert, now fourteen, and Allan, ten, found streams where they could inveigle their father into helping them build dams and canals to provide falls so their water wheels and boats would move.

Lou enjoyed watching the trio, happy with their construction projects, and she liked the pungent smell of the smoke as they helped her cook over the campfires. We are a family again, she thought.

She constantly searched Washington for more convenient living quarters and by the fall the family was more comfortably established at 1701 Massachusetts Avenue. The boys were enrolled in the Friends School, which was within walking distance.

"There is room enough in the yard for a good war garden," Lou told the boys, "and you can help plant it next spring."

"Why do we want a garden?" asked Allan.

"Because food is next in importance to military action during war," explained his mother. "Your father is trying to squeeze out enough foodstuff from the United States, Canada, and the West Indies to help feed the Allied armies as well as our own men in service."

"That is why Dad said agriculture is a munitions industry," contributed Herbert.

"Yes," continued his mother, "and there are only two things we can do to meet this increased need for food. We have to increase our production and decrease our consumption, especially of those foods that can be shipped to the soldiers. Also, some food must go to the starving Belgian mothers and children."

Herbert Hoover was unhappy about the insufficient amount of food available and he enlisted his wife's help.

"I'm opposed to rationing food," he said, "because that worked out badly in Europe. Can't you go out and stir up the women to join the effort voluntarily?"

Lou swallowed hard. "I still don't like making speeches," she replied, "but I'll try."

She appeared in New York in October, to plead the cause of food conservation in behalf of suffering Belgian mothers and American boys in the overseas units. "No letup in food saving must be allowed," she said. "There is some individual who is unknowingly dependent upon you for life; maybe a soldier in the trenches, maybe a little child or a peasant woman. They will not have anything to eat next spring if we do not think of them now."

Lou Hoover did her best to sell the idea of food conservation to other women. She left no stone unturned to involve everyone concerned with food in the movement. She helped to enlist the housewives, public eating places, wholesalers, and retailers, to become card-carrying members of the Food Administration.

In a great patriotic appeal to many sources across the country, the cooperation of the entire American nation was gradually secured to conserve the food supply. Wheatless and meatless days were arranged. Each cooperating member of the Food Administration was given a certificate and asked to sign a pledge and follow the rules. Twenty million members signed up. The rules were all directed toward eliminating waste by reducing unnecessary consumption. Membership cards carried the following: "Go back to simple food, simple clothes, simple pleasures. Pray hard, work hard, sleep and play hard. Do it all courageously and cheerfully. We have a victory to win." The continuation of the war depended partly upon the amount of food that conservation could inspire to the Allied armies.

The cooperative system worked well. Lou's confidence in the ability of the American people to carry through was expressed by her husband's public statement:

The whole foundation of democracy lies in the individual initiative of its people and their willingness to serve the interests of the nation with complete self-effacement in the time of emergency. I hold that Democracy can yield to discipline and that we can solve this food problem for our own people and for our allies largely by voluntary action. To have done so will have been a greater service than our immediate objective, for we have demonstrated the rightness of our faith and our ability to defend ourselves without being Prussianized.

"Food will win the war" became a national slogan, and the conservation measures introduced a new verb into the language, to "Hooverize."

In her own home, Lou practiced what she preached. She cut down on the meat ration, banished wheat, eliminated pork, did without sweets, and encouraged cleaning up plates at the table. "I'm doing just what every other woman is who signed the pledge," she said. "I follow instructions of no cream or butter or lard. We use corn oil, corn bread, poultry, sea foods, and game."

Mary, the cook, had to be educated to see why Lou served such simple food to "quality folks" in Washington. When the boys gave a Halloween party, Mary argued fiercely, "I just have to bake them some cookies for the party."

"No, they will like popcorn just as well," replied Lou.

With Mary's help, Lou Hoover experimented with cereals and vegetables and invented in her own kitchen a number of the wheatless and meatless recipes that she urged upon the housewives of the country in her many speeches.

In the wintertime, Lou planned the Sunday excursions to nearby snow-covered hills for sledding or to a good skating pond where the boys were allowed to build bonfires to keep warm after their vigorous exercise. The whole family enjoyed these outings.

The Hoovers' house, always full of guests, usually included the boys' friends. Because she always valued the friendship of young people, she often brought young Westerners East to give them experience working in Washington. At different times, she brought several young women from California to be her secretaries. Her sister Jean's children, Janet and Delano Large, both had opportunities to live in Washington.

In December 1917, when Allan became ill, she brought her speaking engagements to an abrupt end. She enlisted the aid of her Stanford classmate and friend, Dr. Ray Lyman Wilbur, who decided that Allan needed an appendectomy.

"Dick Follis is the right surgeon," said Dr. Wilbur. So Allan's parents took him to Baltimore where Dr. Richard Follis performed the surgery at Mt. Vernon Hospital.

Lou devoted the next few weeks to taking care of her son, and not until he was back on the healthy list did she return to her public service.

Her interests were myriad, but always the work of philanthropic, welfare, and youth organizations interested her most.

"We need a leader for Scout Troop VIII," pleaded Mrs. Nicholas Brady, president of the Girl Scout Council. "Will you help us, Mrs. Hoover?"

"Of course I will," promised Lou, "and I'll turn over

my yard on Massachusetts Avenue for the troop to culti-
vate a war garden."

Early spring of 1918 saw Scout Leader Hoover in her
garden actively directing the girls in the planting of plots
of vegetables. Later, she pointed with pride to the newspaper statement: "Girl Scout war gardens in Washington,
D.C., are making a real contribution to the food-conserva-
tion program of this area."

Lou was glad to take an active interest in the Girl Scout
movement at this time, partly because of her love for
young people and partly because she was so completely
in sympathy with the character-building purposes of the
organization. War needs of the country made Lou a strong
advocate of training girls to develop vigor, fearlessness,
and initiative. Also, her love of the outdoors made her
eager that American girls should have the best opportunities possible for knowing and appreciating what that
could mean.

Merely lending her name to an organization or movement to build prestige was never her pattern, and the
wife of the Food Administrator put in many hours of
hard work helping Scout troops to start gardens. She accompanied girls on their hikes, took part in their ceremonies, attended regional conferences, and visited girls
in their summer camps. She became a member of the
Scout Council in Washington, as well as leader of Troop
VIII.

Looking backward, although Girl Scouts as an organization was not known in the United States until 1912, Lou
Hoover had been described as being a "lone scout" herself during her zestful childhood full of out-of-doors interests. So it was natural that she should be attracted to
the Girl Scout movement, and she said, "I see three funda-

mental *goods* in it. It teaches play, individual helpfulness, and citizenship."

She explained to Troop VIII:

> The Scout program is not to be likened to a school, where certain things must be taught and learned in large groups. The basic work unit is the patrol, never more than eight, sometimes only four girls. And what the patrols decide is the decision of the troop. Sometimes a captain who loves biology takes the girls out to observe wild life, where they camp, sleep, hike, and cook out-of-doors. Sometimes the patrol devotes itself to folk dancing and semaphore signaling. Girls of all economic levels are thrown together and wear a common uniform. The intimacy of the life in common with her partol thaws out a girl's self-consciousness and helps her develop initiative and personality.

Lou understood and made common cause with her "teen" age girls. She told the council,

> "I believe Girl Scouting is the best method of self-expression for girls; it makes them want to do things they should do. I consider it one of the most worth-while things on which I can spend that part of my day which is not imperatively demanded by my individual responsibilities to my family, my friends, my community, and my nation; for one has certain overt or demanding duties to all of these."

If one phase of Girl Scouting appealed to her more than another, it would be difficult to say which it was, although she loved the camping which reminded her of her younger days with her father. She told the Scout executives with great satisfaction, "More girls take the Homemaking badge than any other." But she also liked to take part in folk dancing and square dancing with the girls, all wearing low-heeled shoes and swinging their partners on the open grass when possible. Of course, all of the phases of nature study appealed to her greatly. She went on long walks over hills and meadows with her girls, looking for birds, flowers, and trees, and told them, "A picnic supper with stories and stunts around the camp-fire I consider an ideal way to spend an evening."

In addition to her Girl Scout activities, the problems of the feminine war workers in finding suitable housing commanded Mrs. Hoover's interest. Thousands of women and girls had flocked to Washington to do war work. Realizing the influence of good living conditions on the health and morale of this army of girls and women, Lou Hoover told her husband, "We must secure appropriate housing, adequate food at a reasonable cost, and opportunities for wholesome recreation for them. Why couldn't we start by organizing the women employees of the Food Administration into a girls' club, and rent inexpensive living quarters for them?"

"Go ahead," Mr. Hoover approved, "and I'll help any way I can."

She insisted that a large cafeteria, serving inexpensive but good food, be established in the new Food Administration Building. This cafeteria became so popular with other government employees as well that, with Lou Hoover's careful financing, there was a nice profit to be used to develop other facilities for the women war workers.

Mrs. Hoover was planning a recreation area for these women when the news came from Europe in March 1918 that the Bolsheviks, then in control, had pulled Russia out of the war and had made a separate peace with Germany. As a result, many German divisions, released from fighting Russia, were being thrown into the Western Front to

Mrs. Herbert Hoover served as National President of the Girl Scouts. She took an active and inspiring part in the work of this fine organization for many years.

The grandparents and parents of Lou Henry Hoover. (Above) *Phineas Weed and Jenny Weed.* (Below) *Mr. and Mrs. Charles D. Henry, in Monterey, around 1900.*

(Above) *Lou Henry at the age of nine,
with her sister Jean, seventeen months, in
Waterloo, Iowa, November, 1883.* (Right)
*At ten, Lou Henry was already devoted to
outdoor sports.*

The busy, happy Stanford College days of Lou Henry and Herbert Hoover, about 1896. (Above) Snapshots in a family album show Lou Henry as chief cook, aided by Marian Dale, for a campfire meal up Carmel Valley; in the chemistry laboratory; and on the archery field. (Right) Young Herbert Hoover shared in many of these activities.

Lou Henry Hoover was perfectly at home in many lands. (Below) Sharing a traditional Japanese tea with her sister Jean, in Yokahama, in 1901. (Left) In Australia with her small son, Herbert, Junior, in 1905.

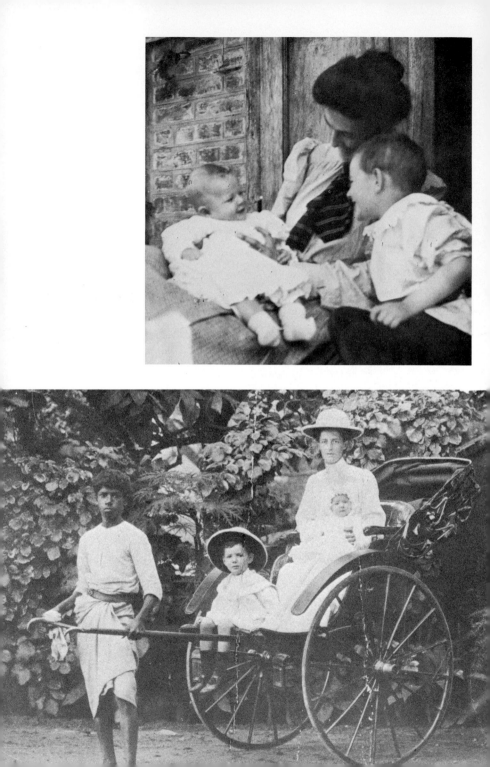

In 1907, the Hoover family were in Burma. (Left above) Mrs. Herbert Hoover with her two young sons, Herbert, Junior, and Allan. (Left below) The boys taking a ride with their nurse.

Mr. and Mrs. Herbert Hoover turned into typical tourists and fed the pigeons with Mr. and Mrs. Edgar Rickard, in St. Mark's Square, Venice, in 1913.

The Hoovers enjoyed doing things together, both while traveling and at home—wherever that might currently be. (Below) *The Hoover family aboard the* Olympia, *in 1918.* (Above) *Allan and Herbert, Junior, with their devoted companion, Rags, in 1920.*

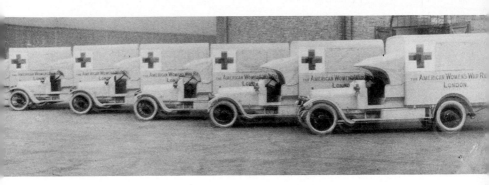

Mrs. Herbert Hoover was always deeply concerned about the welfare of the war wounded. (Above) She was instrumental in securing this fleet of motor ambulances, given by the American Women's War Relief Fund to the British War Office for use at the battlefront, in 1915. (Below) In 1929, she and President Hoover warmly welcomed disabled veterans at a garden party, held on the grounds of the White House, in Washington, D.C.

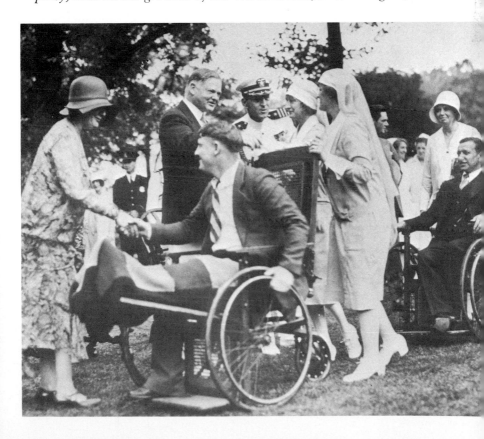

No matter whether it was simple or elaborate, located in far-off China or in the United States, Lou Henry Hoover always managed to make a true home for her family. (Above) *The Hoover-Henry cottage in Monterey, California, in 1902.* (Below) *The Hoover campus residence on San Juan Hill, result of many years of dreaming and planning for their ideal home.*

(Above) *Three generations of the Hoover family are welcomed by neighbors to their San Juan home, in 1928.* (Below) *Lou Henry Hoover received an honorary degree from Whittier College in 1928. She is accompanied by President Dexter and her son Allan.*

(Above) *Mrs. Herbert Hoover, perfect White House hostess, in the Oval Room of the White House, in 1932, with her ever-present charitable knitting.* (Below) *President and Mrs. Herbert Hoover entertained the famous aviatrix, Amelia Earhart Putnam, and her husband, the publisher, George Palmer Putnam, in the White House, on June 22, 1938.* (Opposite) *President and Mrs. Herbert Hoover.*

With best wishes. Lou Henry Hoover

Herbert Hoover.

*Mrs. Hoover found great delight in the company of her beloved grand-
children. (Below) Here she is enjoying Allan, Junior, and Andy, children
of her son, Allan. (Above) The Hoover family group includes, left to right,
Herbert, Junior; his wife Margaret, with their son, Peter; Mrs. Hoover,
holding their lively daughter, Peggy Ann; Herbert Hoover, Senior; and his
son, Allan.*

(Above) *Lou Henry Hoover was ever an enthusiastic and expert horsewoman.* (Below) *The living room of Rapidan Camp, near Washington, D.C., favorite weekend retreat of the Hoovers and their fortunate guests. It was built by them and later presented to the United States Government.*

Lou Henry Hoover, gracious and gallant First Lady of the United States.

fight the Americans. In the months of general stepping up of the war effort which followed, Lou gave much of her time to providing recreation for women war workers.

When school was out, Herbert, Jr., and Allan worked in their mother's "victory garden" and also joined with other young people in selling Liberty Bonds.

Herbert came home triumphant one day to announce to his mother, "My Scout troop outsold all the others in town for this whole week."

Lou praised him and then asked, "How would you and Allan like to spend a few weeks this summer at your uncle Theodore's Rancho Del Oso in the Santa Cruz Mountains?"

"Fine," replied Herbert. "It won't be so hot out there."

The boys were allowed to travel to California without their parents.

During that summer and fall of 1918, Washington was engulfed in a highly virulent death-dealing, world-wide, pandemic of influenza. People were seized with the illness suddenly, like Mary, the Hoovers' cook, who left to go shopping and ended up in the hospital two hours later severely ill.

More than half of the Food Administration workers were stricken and business ground practically to a standstill. The hospitals were overflowing and Lou Hoover was called upon to organize nursing care for the Food Administration women workers in their own Girls' Club dormitory. Most of these women were a long way from their homes and she arranged to notify their families in all cases of illness and sometimes, unfortunately, of death, throughout the hot summer months.

"I'm thankful that Herbert and Allan are away on a California ranch and not in contact with these Washington crowds," Lou told Bert. "Maybe the flu isn't so bad out there."

"It is out there, too," replied Bert. "This pandemic has already slaughtered 300,000 people in the United States and 800,000 in Europe, which adds up to more people than have been killed in the war this year."

In the midst of all the worry and concern for the influenza victims came the amazing news on October 12, 1918, that the Germans had appealed to President Wilson for an armistice. Lou Hoover could hardly believe it and she asked her husband, "Could it be a trick to gain time?"

"No," was the reply, "I think they have come to the end of their rope. But we will have to watch what happens in Europe now."

"There have been four years of this frightful war," said Lou, "and the toll has been terrific."

"Yes," Bert told her sadly. "Over 8 million men have been killed out of 60 million fighters, and unknown millions of other people have died of starvation or disease directly due to the war. Nineteen nations have been actively engaged in it, eleven declared war but did not fight, and only nineteen remained neutral."

"Oh, when will nations ever learn to live in peace?" sighed Lou. "If this war is really over," she began, brightening, as she laid her hand on his arm, "at least you will be out from under the heavy burdens of your own public service and we can build our permanent home on our Stanford hill."

Bert smiled at her understandingly.

Finally, on November 11, 1918, the armistice was signed, and Lou Hoover was aglow with the general excitement and joy which swept over the country.

"The prospect of peace is precious," she told the boys,

safely back in Washington after their stay in the West. "Perhaps now we can live as a family."

However, another separation was in store. On November 17, only six days after the armistice, Lou Hoover and the two boys stood on a dock in New York watching the father of the family embark on the *Olympic* bound for Europe, to start two more years of work on relief and reconstruction.

The specter of starving people was emerging all over Europe and Congress had appropriated relief money. President Wilson promptly appointed Herbert Hoover to administer the American Relief funds and General Pershing dubbed Mr. Hoover "Food Regulator of the World."

Many of his old CRB (Commission for Relief in Belgium) friends who had worked under Herbert Hoover in the American Food Administration, joined him now to help distribute food and establish the machinery of economic rehabilitation in Europe.

Edgar Rickard was appointed head of the American Food Administration in the United States and began to reorganize it on a peace-time basis.

After seeing her husband off, Mrs. Hoover helped many of the women war workers to find new employment and rejoiced with others who welcomed their husbands returning from the battlefields of Europe.

Lou Hoover and her boys returned to Palo Alto in time to spend the Thanksgiving holidays with her parents. Herbert enrolled at the Palo Alto High School and Allan at the Campus School.

Throughout the United States, building projects were encouraged to help the national economy, so Lou Hoover felt patriotic as she turned her attention toward the building of their dream home. She now made her own preliminary architectural drawings for a house adapted to the sloping hilltop on San Juan Hill, overlooking the Santa Clara Valley. These sketches included features of several homes in other lands where the family had lived.

Before school was out in the spring of 1919, sixteen-year-old Herbert decided that he wanted to work that summer. He told his mother, "Uncle Theodore needs some men to work on his ranch. He'll be going down there as soon as spring quarter is over at Stanford. He wants me to paint fences for him and I want to do it."

Ray Lyman Wilbur, then president of Stanford, had appointed Theodore Hoover professor and executive head of the Department of Mining and Metallurgy earlier that year.

"All right," Lou Hoover agreed. "A summmer at the ranch and some manual labor will be good for you," and then she thought with a pang, he will be old enough to leave home before we get our own home built.

As soon as school was out, Mrs. Hoover headed for Paris to be with her husband. Allan accompanied her. The boy's experience with the war are best described in Herbert Hoover's *Memoirs:*

In 1919, a few weeks before the end, Mrs. H. came to Paris with Allan to be with me for a little while and to accompany me home. She brought about a union of Allan and General Pershing's son Warren, both of whom were then about twelve years old. She attached to them a French lady to improve their French and the general contributed a sergeant who served as enforcement officer and tourist agent. They roamed the old battlefields and Paris generally. Allan undertook an important collection of arms from the spots where they had been used. Among them was an aerial torpedo which he had picked up on the Chemin des Dames. His enforcement agency carefully unloaded it and Allan prized it highly. One night a group of generals dined with us and one of them inspected Allan's collection. When he came to the aerial torpedo he expressed vivid alarm. He insisted on taking it at once from the hotel. He had it dropped carefully into the Seine. No explanation that we could give satisfied Allan as to the general's character as a gentleman or his competence as a military man.

Early in September, Allan and his parents returned on the *Aquitania*. They were met by young Herbert in New York. As Lou looked down on the dock and saw her bronzed, broad-shouldered elder son, she thought, he has become a self-sufficient young man.

She was happy when he greeted her with, "We will have just time enough for a camping trip in the mountains before school begins."

Lou longed to get started for the West immediately but the family was held up in New York for a day while the Engineers of America honored Mr. and Mrs. Hoover with a big public dinner and reception before they could head for California.

Even the few weeks in California were disrupted. The Hoovers had just settled down on the Stanford campus, after a brief but delightful camping trip in the High Sierra, when King Albert, Queen Elizabeth, and Crown Prince Leopold of Belgium arrived as guests of the United States government. They were the first official guests of the nation by congressional invitation for nearly one hundred years. Because President Wilson was ill, he asked the Hoovers to entertain the royal visitors. Lou could not attend the parade up Market Street for the San Francisco reception at the Civic Center on October 8, because Allan had fallen out of a tree that morning and broken his arm. Mayor Rolph accepted a royal decoration in behalf of the city of San Francisco. Later that day, at the Palace Hotel, King Albert conferred the Cross of Chevalier, Order of

Leopold, on Lou Hoover, in recognition of her relief work in behalf of Belgium.

Mrs. Hoover received the award graciously. "What is there to say?" she asked. "I have done nothing extraordinary nor anything more than a woman should do for the man she loves. I have been deeply interested in Mr. Hoover's work and have tried to be of whatever assistance I could. My chief hobbies are my husband and our sons."

She told King Albert that she and her husband treasured most of all the thousands of letters they had received from the grateful children of Belgium.

When the royal visitors had departed, Lou and Bert Hoover plunged into the organization of some of the mountains of printed material arriving at the Hoover Library on War, Revolution, and Peace, which had been founded at Stanford University as a result of "Operation Pack Rat." At Herbert Hoover's request, made before he left Europe, General Pershing had detailed fifteen history professors from the armed forces to gather all possible war records from throughout Europe.

"This valuable documentary material on the causes of war should be analyzed so mankind may know how to build the peace," said Bert.

The Christmas holidays of 1919 were glorious days for Lou. She had her family all together, she was in California, she was actively planning with her husband for their permanent home, and the world was at peace. It was a very thankful Christmas.

When at long last, early in 1920, the "permanent" Hoover home on the Stanford campus was arriving at the blueprint stage on the drawing board of Arthur B. Clark, the architect, they saw their own ideas and designs taking shape. Sitting at her desk with the blueprints in front of her, Lou told Allan, "Our house must be an elastic thing, never entirely finished, always growing with the needs of our family and be adaptable to our changing needs."

"Can we have a swimming pool?" asked Allan.

His mother pushed her hair back and quickly sketched in a pool on one of the terraces.

The type of construction on San Juan Hill made for flexibility. Fireproof throughout, the external architecture, with its flat roofs and terraces, reflected some Hopi Indian design, modified by Algerian domestic features gathered from the shores of the Mediterranean. Lou Hoover, herself, designed the fireplace on one terrace and insisted that the three levels of terraces all be furnished for out-of-door living with a tennis court on one and a swimming pool on another for the boys.

In clear weather the terraces commanded a view of the campanile at Berkeley, a long stretch of East Bay hills, the end of the bay to the south, and Mt. Hamilton in the distance. She arranged the modern interior to allow both family and guests privacy or room to congregate, as they desired.

The house, even before it was completely finished in 1921, was forever overflowing with crowds of young people who enjoyed the atmosphere of comfort and happiness. Herbert, Jr., who attended Palo Alto High School, liked to give gay informal parties that often spilled out of the living room for dancing on a terrace. The school year slipped by rapidly.

Herbert and Allan both earned their own spending money. When Herbert wanted a motorcar, his mother encouraged him to buy the materials a little at a time and build his own car. When it was finished, he asked her, "Will you take a ride with me?"

"Of course," she replied promptly, climbing in. "I knew

you could do it, but can't you take out some of the noise?"

It was necessary to continue feeding destitute European children and in July 1920 the American Relief Administration was organized. It was composed of the Red Cross, Friends Service Committee, Jewish Joint Distribution Committee, Knights of Columbus, the YWCA, the YMCA, and the Federal Council of Chruches.

Lou Hoover agreed it was logical that her husband be appointed to oversee this program, but her heart sank at the thought of leaving their new home. I'll just have to live in two different places again, she thought.

Herbert Hoover rented an apartment in a New York hotel and established his office at 42 Broadway, from which he administered the European Children's Relief program. Lou alternated her time between her husband in New York and her sons in their California home.

In spite of her divided allegiance, she was thoroughly interested in her husband's relief program, and, as an experienced fund raiser, was drafted to help raise the badly needed money. Collecting relief money with new ideas, she dramatized the drive in many parts of the country by banquets to an Invisible Guest.

At these "banquets," rough board tables were set with tin dishes for the guests. An empty high chair was always placed at the head of the table and Red Cross nurses or college girls served the same kind of food being given to undernourished children in Europe. People attending these dinners contributed from $1.00 to $500 per plate. Lou Hoover helped arrange one of these "banquets" on December 29, 1920, in New York City, where 1,000 guests paid $1,000 per plate to attend. On that night a special collection brought in another million dollars in pledges and John D. Rockefeller gave the third million, which put this particular drive well over the top.

Herbert and Allan joined their parents for the Christmas holidays in New York and Lou planned some family activities which took Bert away from his office to be with his boys. They went to see Lionel Barrymore play *Macbeth* on Broadway, and *Abie's Irish Rose* at the Music Hall. Lou Hoover was happy to have her family all together once more.

She returned to Palo Alto with the boys and entered enthusiastically into their activities. Herbert was enjoying his senior year at high school. He was popular socially, and entered into extracurricular activities. Allan was finishing up at the Campus School.

Lou thought longingly, it can't be too much longer until Bert will complete the relief program and come home.

But even before his inauguration, President Harding appointed Herbert Hoover Secretary of Commerce. On March 4, 1921, Lou and Bert Hoover watched a robust and genial Warren G. Harding inaugurated President of the United States, contrasting mightily as he stood beside the physically shattered Woodrow Wilson.

IX

CABINET WIFE

•

1921–1923

DOWN THE BLOCK from the residence of the Woodrow
Wilsons in Washington, D.C., stood a comfortable colonial house with an acre of grounds in which great oak trees
grew. Early in March 1921, Lou and Bert Hoover wandered through its empty rooms.

"I like the large dining room," Lou said. "We're going
to have to do more entertaining now." She walked to a
window and looked out. "I only wish there were some
way we could eat out-of-doors, too," she said wistfully,
"the way we do at home."

"California will always be home to you, won't it?" her
husband asked with an understanding smile.

"Of course," Lou replied quickly, and then seeing the
look in his eyes, she went to put her cheek against his.
"Home is where you are," she whispered, little realizing
that where Herbert Hoover would be that year and for
the next twelve was in Washington, D.C.

As Lou Hoover stood looking out the window, in her
thoughts she recalled vividly that day in the previous
January when Daniel Guggenheim had offered Bert a

122

partnership in the largest mining firm in the world with guaranteed annual remuneration of $500,000. She had been delighted, longing for the freedom and the kind of life it promised her family. She remembered now how her dream bubble had burst on February 21 when Bert was asked to become Secretary of Commerce. His decision to accept the government position was far more altruistic than most Americans knew. The war had greatly reduced the wealth of the Hoovers, as Bert had neglected his own business affairs to devote his time to humanity. In addition, Lou had contributed much of her own money to help needy people suffering the devastations of war. While the Hoovers were not poor, they were no longer wealthy. But Bert deeply desired to serve his country. Lou was in full sympathy with him and agreed that her husband should go into public service. It seemed appropriate because of his world-wide experience with peoples of all nations and his perspective on the war. She accepted the all-too-familiar fact that public life would leave him little time for family life or recreational activities.

Lou went to work immediately to convert the house at 2300 S Street into a home. It was located on a hillside overlooking part of Washington. She promptly planted bright flowers in long boxes, to be placed on the railing of the large porch across the back of the house, where she served meals out-of-doors, California style, during the spring and summer and early fall. Gourd vines trailing over the steps and porch rails added a note of coolness. An Oriental influence found its way into the peaceful garden with a pond where wide-tailed Japanese goldfish were placed.

"We don't like to look out on brick walls," she told a visitor who had wondered at the naturalness of the place so close to the center of the city. "We like the wild ground cover, so all we've done is make a rambling walk or two and put in a few rustic seats. It is a fine playground for children and pets."

The inside of the spacious house Lou furnished very simply. The homiest room was Bert's study. Clustered in front of the fireplace were comfortable chairs and a lounge, suggesting a prized spot for retreat and rest. Bookcases lined two walls. Chosen from many tributes, Lou placed in a position of honor on top of a bookcase the unique gift from Belgium, a richly carved wooden box containing a parchment in the Belgian language, expressing the warm gratitude of the Belgian people toward Herbert Hoover. The box rested on a silken pillowcase elaborately embroidered by Belgian children. But an American touch had been added. The back of the pillowcase was an Oregon flour sack with the lettering still there. It was one of those many sacks of flour that "Hooverism" had inspired and that American families had done without in order to help save the children of Belgium from starvation.

The Hoover boys had numerous assorted pets. During spring vacation, Herbert built a house for his dog near the back porch. Allan took special delight in his mother's garden. He made a birdbath and hung gourds in the trees, where he kept seeds for the birds which flocked in every day. Among his other pets were a cat and dog, two small alligators, land turtles, and two ducks, which he trained to sit on the front porch. His mother enjoyed all his pets except the alligators. When she encountered them in her bathtub one day, she said firmly, "Allan, you know that I want you to have pets, but these alligators you will just have to keep at the zoo."

The following fall, Allan remained in Washington and

attended the Friends School, but Herbert returned to his uncle Theodore's home so he could graduate with his class at Palo Alto High School in the spring of 1921. He was ready to enter Stanford that fall when he was eighteen.

The summer was marred for Lou Hoover by the death of her mother. She hastened to Monterey and spent several days with her father and sister, Jean Henry Large. The sisters tried to help their father to make plans for his future, living with one or the other of them, but Charles Henry elected to remain in Monterey.

Home for the Hoover family was now Washington, D.C. Lou had been right about the amount of entertaining she would have to do as a Cabinet wife. She was a gracious hostess for all manner of people. In warm weather, when there were too many guests for the porch, the overflow ate from tables in the lovely, natural garden.

A friend once commented on Lou's constant entertaining. She responded, "I never entertain; I just ask people to come in to see us and we enjoy each other."

Another friend described her, "Mrs. Hoover is like her garden in that it seems so beautifully out of the rush and noise of the city, yet it is in the heart of it. That is, she is so seemingly untouched by all that is going on around her, yet is so vitally and keenly interested and involved in everything worth while."

Lou kept open house at 2300 S Street during all of the eight years she lived there. Often it looked like an all-nations assembly, for the guests were the Hoover family's friends from Europe and Asia as well as from many parts of the United States. Nearly always present were other cabinet members and congressmen.

Lou Hoover preferred to entertain informally, but occasionally they had formal parties. Late in March 1922, she gave the usual official Cabinet dinner for President and Mrs. Harding. The society columns reported that the other guests included director of the National Research Council, Vernon Kellogg and his wife; Aurelia Henry Reinhardt, president of Mills College; Hugh Gibson, American Minister to Poland and his Belgian bride; and Mr. and Mrs. Edward T. Pickard of the Department of Commerce. "The hostess wore a handsome gown of black velvet-embossed chiffon made with a surplice bodice filled in with a vest of lovely lace. Her skirt was draped on the side in a long-line effect."

Mrs. Hoover enjoyed wearing her frilly feminine dresses for social occasions just as much as she did her tweedy outfits for Girl Scout events or for riding in the park.

One evening later that spring, while the Hoover family and a few close friends were in the midst of their evening meal, two senators and their wives arrived for dinner. Bert looked at Lou sheepishly. "You know, I invited them this morning and forgot to tell you," he confessed.

Lou was equal to the occasion. Laughingly, she hustled the original guests into another room, bound them to secrecy, and directed her husband, "You meet the senators and keep them busy for a while." Then she took an SOS message to the understanding cook and in due course both groups of guests came to the dining room together and sat down to a fresh dinner.

Her new official duties did not crowd out Lou Hoover's old interests. Her maternal instincts had reached out to the girls of the whole nation when she adopted the Girl Scouts during her Food Administration days. She enjoyed the technical and executive part of Scouting and now tried to build preparedness for life into the Girl Scout program in Washington.

"The ideal of Girl Scout training," she explained to one of her luncheon guests, "is to develop wise and resourceful citizens by exploring trails which lead out of the pleasant fields of childhood to the broad and teeming highways of adult life."

She was concerned about the emerging new types of women. The "roaring twenties" produced three characteristic new types: the sophisticate, the flapper, and the career girl. Lou believed in the inherent idealism of youth and very logically tried to give leadership to the character-building organizations.

A teenage girl, to say nothing of twenty of them at once, stumped many leaders, but not Lou Hoover. As an active member of her troop, she was interested in the same things that interested them. She loved their good times and laughed with them. In fact, she proved to be far more than their equal in most of the games they played.

All through a ten-day Girl Scout camp in the Ozark Mountains, Lou Hoover led discussions, shared in the duties of the camp, participated in hiking and out-of-door cooking, was out with the first for before-breakfast bird walks, never missed a flag raising, shot moving pictures for recreation, analyzed rocks found thereabout, and knitted in meetings to have something to do. At night, she wrote reports of each day's progress and was as full of jokes in the evening as in the morning. Elected president of the National Council of Girl Scouts at the eighth annual convention held in Savannah, Georgia, on January 26, 1922, she said:

"Few girls receive domestic training these days. A girl may be a good stenographer, bookkeeper, law clerk or politician, but few know how to bake a cake, darn a sock or do any of the thousand-and-one little domestic tricks their grandmothers could perform as second nature."

One of Lou's first activities as president was to issue a call for 10,000 young women to train to become Girl Scout leaders, saying that only through them could the organization meet the demand of the girls themselves. The Scouts joined with the Girl Reserves of the YWCA in a leadership training program and enlisted many new leaders.

At one of the training sessions Lou said,

"Girl Scouts seem to have a better time working than playing, and a better time working for others than for themselves. Those I have known get a tremendous exaltation from serving others; and a frequent result of the voluntary cooperation and comradeship in Girl Scout activities is the development of thought and helpfulness for other people. This makes our girls better homemakers, better citizens, better friends. Individually, it tends toward a keener mind, a finer character, and a happier self."

From her college days on, Lou had always promoted physical fitness, and the Scout program gave her exceptional opportunities in this field. She was glad that the vogue of the pale and languid young lady had passed into discard and that, instead of croquet, she was beginning to engage in all sorts of organized athletics. So it was natural that Lou Hoover should be made vice president of the National Amateur Athletic Federation—its only woman officer. She worked actively with this organization to develop physical education and mass-play opportunities for men and women, boys and girls of all ages.

At a meeting called in Washington in April 1923, Lou Hoover organized the women's division as the National

Woman's Athletic Association and built in some safe-
guards for girls.

She was opposed to publicity and expensive trophies
for women athletes. "Motivation of competitors in athletic activities should be to maintain the amateur spirit
of play for play's sake," she declared. "Awarding of valuable prizes is detrimental to this objective," she continued,
"and publicity for women should stress the sport and not
the individual or group competitors. But even though
girls play for fun they should always have efficient medical examinations before entering athletic events."

Lou indicated that she thought healthful athletics
would tend to lessen girls' interest in "spooning" but was
roundly challenged by a group of Baltimore women who
did not agree that "petting" would be ended by athletics.

Colleges began to recognize Lou Hoover's contribution
to girls and women through the Scout program and in
the field of athletics. On May 14, 1923, Lou was awarded
an honorary Master of Arts degree from Mills College
at Oakland, California.[1] Following this, she had a few
happy days with her boys in Palo Alto. Allan lived with
his uncle Theodore on the Stanford campus and was attending Palo Alto High School, while Herbert, a Junior
at Stanford, lived in a dormitory.

Mrs. Hoover would gladly have spent her days with
her family, her friends, and her Girl Scouts, but inevitably
she became involved in politics. She addressed 400 Republican women of Pennsylvania in Philadelphia at a
Ritz-Carlton Hotel luncheon late in May of that same
year, 1923.

"Women should get into politics. They should take a
more active part in civic affairs, give up some of their time

1 See Appendix 4.

devoted to pleasure for their duty as citizens. Whether we are wanted in politics or not, we are here to stay and the only force that can put us out is that which gave us the vote. The vote itself is not a perfect utility. It is perfected in the way in which it is used."

Later that spring, Lou was honored at a dinner given by the League of Women Voters. The audience saw a slender woman in a very becoming costume of platinum-gray duvetyn, made with a long-waisted gown and a loose overwrap, trimmed in rows of silk braid, in a shade darker than the material. Her gray velvet hat, which had a high crown and medium brim, was trimmed with shaded gray feathers. On that occasion, Lou stressed the importance of the League.

"If all women have not the time to give personal services to the ideals of the League, they can at least see that the proper laws are enacted by voting at the polls. One of the principal purposes of the League is to study and clarify for the benefit of women voters the meaning of the government and its machinations. As a strictly nonpartisan organization the League can be and will be more of a power behind the throne than were it to enter the field as a third party. It is not only for nonpartisan voters but for those in either party. "We need women as well as men in politics. To make a party whole there should be as many feminine as masculine minds."

On a hot day late in June, Herbert Hoover, trying to maintain an air of nonchalance, asked his wife, "How would you like to go to Alaska and cool off? President Harding has asked us to go with him on a trip." Lou was fond of the President and of his lady and she responded with enthusiasm.

The presidential party boarded their ship in Seattle on July 3, 1923. Lou thoroughly enjoyed seeing the grandeur of Alaska's snow-capped peaks and vast glaciers as the vessel cruised through the beautiful Inside Passage.

"Why does President Harding play bridge all day long and into the night, constantly surrounded by the same group of men?" Lou asked her husband.

"He is beginning to find out about the dishonest schemes of some of his alleged friends," replied Bert, "and is worried sick about a scandal in his administration."

Lou observed how day by day President Harding became more nervous and fatigued. She learned from Florence Harding that the receptions, parades, and speeches at every town along the way to Fairbanks, by boat, train, and automobile, were keeping him under great strain. On the way home, several speeches on a hot day in Vancouver, late in July, proved too much and Warren Harding asked friends to appear for him.

Lou heard him falter in his Seattle speech on July 27, and saw him rushed to their special train, where Dr. Joel Boone, Navy surgeon, diagnosed a heart attack.

"The President will be too sick to make a speech in San Francisco, so what will he do?" Lou Hoover wanted to know.

"The newspapers will get his speech," replied her husband, "because he asked me to write one for him."

Herbert Hoover wired ahead to Dr. Ray Lyman Wilbur to meet their special train in San Francisco, with heart specialists ready for consultation. The presidential party went to the Palace Hotel, where the doctors diagnosed a massive heart damage. President Harding died at the hotel on August 2, 1923.

When Lou Hoover heard the news she rushed to Flor-

ence Harding's room and found her weeping. "Don't
leave me," begged the anguished woman.

Mrs. Hoover stayed with Warren Harding's widow almost continuously for many hours after the death of the
President. When questioned by reporters, she declared
that the First Lady was bearing up admirably under the
shock of the tragedy. "Mrs. Harding is perfectly well,"
she reported. "Of course she cries, but there is nothing
like a collapse. She is going to be terribly upset if she
sees in the newspapers that she collapsed."

The two women traveled together on the four-day trip
across the continent to Washington and Lou Hoover
helped Florence Harding to keep up her courage. They
read in the newspapers that Vice President Calvin Coolidge was spending the summer on his Vermont farm,
where there was no telephone. After the delayed news
of President Harding's death reached them, Colonel Coolidge, father of Calvin, administered the oath of office by
oil lamp at 2:47 A.M., to make Calvin Coolidge President
of the United States.

The Harding funeral train reached Washington, D.C.,
on August 7, 1923, and a huge state funeral service was
conducted, followed by burial at Marion, Ohio, the Harding home.

After the ceremonies in Marion, Lou Hoover went to
Palo Alto to have a brief vacation with her boys. Herbert
had been in the Santa Cruz mountains all summer, working at his uncle Theodore's Rancho del Oso (Spanish for
bear), so after a few relaxed days in the campus home, his
mother and brother joined him there. "The Brown House"
was snuggled up against a steep hillside covered with
redwoods. It had elastic walls and sheltered many guests,
including Lou Hoover, but Allan shared "Camp Herbert,"
a nearby lean to, with his brother. Waddell Creek had

cut a canyon through the trees to the ocean, which provided beautiful hiking and picnic spots.

Other guests at Rancho del Oso asked Mrs. Hoover many questions about the government officials in Washington as they read of the congressional investigation of the administration, which was already under way. There were no easy answers.

Lou Hoover hated to end her California holiday, but she also wanted to be with her husband. Back in the capital, the weeks went by rapidly that fall and as usual many demands were made on her time.

She addressed the Columbus Day conference arranged by the United States section of the Pan-American International Women's Committee. She talked about establishing better understanding and better relations among republics by providing a means of acquainting the women of one country with the achievements of those of others. The meeting, held in the magnificent new Pan-American Building, drew many national figures and prominent educators.

Lou Hoover had also helped arrange for speakers on the subject of international understanding to appear on the same day in the capitals of Argentina, Brazil, Chile, Peru, Ecuador, Nicaragua, Guatemala, Costa Rica, Haiti, Cuba, Mexico, Venezuela, and Panama.

As the wife of the Secretary of Commerce, Mrs. Hoover attended many White House parties and naturally she dressed according to the dictates of protocol—and fashion —although she was not inclined to play the Washington society game in a big way. Up to the time of her public life, she had not patronized the beauty parlors and had preferred very simple dress.

The society column of the Washington *Post* frequently described her appearance at social and political functions.

She attended a White House party for the diplomatic corps in December 1923 dressed in a gown of gold-and-black brocade with a generous train, as all gowns for state occasions were expected to have in those days. At another party, she wore a white velvet gown with long, close lines, and her necklace and corsage ornaments were sapphires. There was great latitude in the length of skirts that year and two distinct hemlines, a short one for daytime and a long one for evening. Lou had short crepe and jersey dresses for daytime and enjoyed wearing a sweater over a sleeveless sports dress for some of her Girl Scout activities.

Winter came and Lou planned many festivities for the 1923 Christmas season. Allan came home from Palo Alto High School to spend the holidays with his family in Washington, but Herbert did not have a long enough vacation from Stanford to make the trip.

Allan's clothes reflected men's fashions that year, including a Chesterfield overcoat with wide shoulders, deep lapels, and high pockets. His hat brim was broad and deeply curved. He brought along tweedy casual clothes for sports.

The Hoovers' other house guests for the holidays included Ambassador Hugh Gibson and his Belgian wife, old friends Mr. and Mrs. Edgar Rickard, and Dr. and Mrs. Vernon Kellogg from Palo Alto. Their host especially enjoyed this group, all of whom had worked with his Commission for Relief of Belgium, and could relax and chat with them, although he always tended to be diffident with strangers. On one vacation day Herbert Hoover showed Allan through the intricacies of the Department of Commerce offices and they discussed government agencies.

"How would you like to give a party while you are

here?" Lou Hoover asked her son. "Do you think a paper chase would be fun?"

"That would be fine," replied Allan, "if we can dance afterward."

"Oh, I know just the place," said his mother. "The Pierce Mill Tea House, run for the benefit of the Girl Scouts, is a splendid place to dance and they will serve a good dinner."

On December 28, 1923, the large group of young people invited by Mrs. Hoover and Allan assembled at 3 P.M. at 2300 S Street and followed their leader in a strenuous ramble through Rock Creek Park to the Tea House, where dinner was ready at six.

Lou enjoyed Allan's party as much as he did and went to bed that night feeling happy about her boys and proud of their development and achievements. She knew that Bert was doing what he actually wanted to do and she shared his deep convictions about the significance of service to others. She was content.

X

POLITICS AND PUBLIC SERVICE

•

1924–1928

DURING THE NEXT four years Lou Hoover shuttled back and forth across the continent by train, making a home for her husband in Washington and spending as much time as possible with her sons in Palo Alto. Soon we will finish up in Washington, she thought, and then we can settle down and enjoy our own home on the campus.

But there were many worries. The senior Hoovers were frightened by a growing loss of respect for law in the United States and shocked at the involvement of elected public officials in graft. The Teapot Dome scandal exploded around the country in the spring of 1924. Lou, with shocked repugnance, could not believe the tales of corruption about many men whom she had known in the Harding administration.

Wherever Lou met with groups of women, the talk invariably turned to Teapot Dome. At a luncheon with one of the Cabinet wives, the hostess said, "You are lucky, Mrs. Hoover, because no one ever dreams of accusing your husband of being involved in this mess, but lots of other men are being investigated. They are all big names, too, like Fall, Sinclair, and Doheny."

After much litigation, Albert Fall, Secretary of the Interior, was convicted of leasing Federal oil reserve land at Teapot Dome, Wyoming, to Harry F. Sinclair and also certain California oil lands to Edward L. Doheny. Lou heard that oil interests had lavishly supported Harding's campaign for the presidency. During the investigation, Secretary of the Navy Edwin Denby was condemned for negligence in authorizing transfer of naval oil reserves to the Secretary of the Interior. Edward McLean, who loaned Albert Fall $100,000, lost control of his newspaper, the Washington *Post,* and many others were involved in the affair. Sinclair and Secretary Fall received prison sentences.

President Coolidge demanded Denby's resignation. He also pushed civil action which was successful in the recovery of the leases and damages. Bert told Lou, "President Coolidge's accomplishment will help to restore America's faith in the rulers of the land since careful scrutiny of his strict personal standards uncovered no hint of graft, waste, or extravagance in the President himself."

Lou's characteristic reaction to the whole chaotic situation was to help stir up the women of the country to try to do something about law enforcement. At 1734 N Street, headquarters of the General Federation of Women's Clubs, she helped plan a nationwide campaign. "Women of the country are tired of seeing the laws of our land ignored," she declared.

A conference on law enforcement was called for April 10–11, 1924, in Washington. Five hundred out-of-town delegates from thirty-six states came by special trains and one thousand local women attended. Enthusiasm ran high and the delegates discussed law enforcement in the fullest sense.

Lou Hoover presided at the meetings. In her opening address, she said, "I am heart and soul in sympathy with the women of this country who are trying to promote law observance and law enforcement, and will do everything I can to help. We must arouse the whole country to an understanding of the dangerous significance of continued evasion of law."

President Calvin Coolidge and Secretary of the Navy Curtis D. Wilbur spoke at the opening session. President Coolidge declared, "A revival of old-fashioned respect for the law is essential to the continued security of America."

Tallying the total membership of all the clubs represented, 10 million women backed the Washington conference for enforcement of law. Lou Hoover felt that the conference had been a successful venture in public education and she hoped women everywhere would remember their power at the polls.

Both Lou and Bert Hoover went to Palo Alto in May to cast their votes in the Santa Clara County spring election. Stopping off between trains on her way from her "official" residence in Washington to the Hoover's "real home" in California, Mrs. Hoover spoke at the twenty-eighth annual convention of the National Congress of Mothers and Parent-Teachers Associations in St. Paul, Minnesota. She made a plea to the delegates to help improve public-school conditions in the District of Columbia. She said that because of the poor facilities in the public schools there, she and her husband had preferred to send their son Allan, now a senior, to a high school in California, even though it necessitated a separation from home ties during the year for their son.

After her husband returned to the capital, Lou lingered

a few days in Palo Alto with Herbert and Allan, enjoying their campus home. She persuaded her father to accompany her on the return trip to Washington and to stay for a visit.

Early in June, with a feeling of release and pleasure, Lou left again for Palo Alto to spend the summer with her sons at the brick-terraced home on San Juan Hill.

Being at home merely changed the locale of her activities. On June 13, she gave the graduation address at the Castilleja private school for girls in Palo Alto. The girls were greatly impressed by this gracious woman with her gray hair in soft, old-fashioned waves about her face and her deep blue eyes that were kind but penetrating in their glance. "We can control our lives," she said, "and we need to choose among various lines of service and among various ways of using leisure time, what books are to be read, what athletics enjoyed, and what beautiful memories stored up."

The big excitement of the summer for Lou was the dinner she and her husband gave on San Juan Hill in July to celebrate the engagement of Herbert, Jr., to Margaret Watson, his Stanford classmate. Bert crossed the continent to be present at the dinner and to share in his wife's pleasure at the prospect of a daughter in the family. Margaret was the daughter of Mr. and Mrs. Douglas Watson of San Francisco, and the dinner was strictly a family affair. Lou had known Douglas Watson as a schoolmate since he had graduated from Stanford one year after she did.

Lou told her friends with pride and warm-hearted approval, "Margaret is president of the Woman's Athletic Association at Stanford and a member of Kappa Alpha Theta sorority, and Herbert is vice president of the student body and member of the Men's Council. Both young people are seniors now with one more year ahead of them before they graduate from Stanford and we are pleased that they intend to complete their courses before naming the wedding day."

After a few short days, Herbert Hoover returned to Washington. Happy weeks with her boys were terminated in September, when Allan entered Stanford as a freshman and Lou Hoover returned to Washington and multitudes of duties. The fall was as busy as ever. She was soon engaged in a campaign to raise a two-year budget of $97,000 to support the Visiting Nurse Society. Mrs. Hoover praised the organization and said, "The value of the Instructive Visiting Nurses can scarcely be overestimated. I saw much of their work during the war."

Lou Hoover looked forward to Christmas and their traditional family reunion. A unique Christmas card for 1924, designed by Allan, presented each member of the family. It was a two-page folder and on the first inside page were the greetings, "All the Hoovers wish you a Merry Christmas and a Happy New Year and wish they knew what you were doing." On the opposite page were snapshots of each member of the family. First came Rags the dog, and by the side of his picture the words, "Rags reports that Allan is now a freshman." Allan's photograph had a college pennant back of it. Next came the announcement, "Herbert has got engaged," and there was Herbert looking at his fiancée beside him. Margaret was very demure and sweet and Herbert had a very broad smile on his face. Next came Lou Hoover's picture with the words, "Mom is still Girl Scouting." Last came a picture of Herbert Hoover, Sr., reading a letter, with a serious look on his face. The label read, "Dad is quite unchanged."

The holidays went all too fast and soon the boys were

back at college and Lou settled into her own routine in
Washington. Of the Cabinet wives, she was undoubtedly
the busiest, with a record of earnest public service. As a
speaker she was much in demand by women's organizations and colleges, and probably was asked to serve on
more committees and commissions than any other woman
in the United States.

One of her pleasant duties was to attend regional Girl
Scout conferences. Her personal philosophy, worked out
through her own wide experience, was evident in many
of her talks. In this philosophy, the chief element of
leadership was giving something of yourself. When the
Campfire Girls called on her to help them in their building campaign on March 24, 1926, she stated, "Money is
a wonderful thing to have; it makes possible so much
material achievement. But even more important to us
than money are leaders, workers, or rather players in the
same game with us. And what is leadership," she asked,
"but the giving of something which we have acquired in
the years of our experience which those of fewer years
and less experience might enjoy and benefit by?"

Lou Hoover could hardly wait to reach Palo Alto that
spring of 1925, because Herbert would graduate from
Stanford on June 22 and his wedding was set for three
days later. After commencement, everyone focused on
the coming marriage.

"I am happy and excited," Lou Hoover confided to
Margaret's mother, as they worked together on preparations for the wedding. "It will be so wonderful to have
a daughter."

The father of the groom arrived from Washington just
in time for the ceremony and returned shortly afterward.
On June 25, as Lou Hoover watched lovely Margaret
come down the aisle of the Stanford Memorial Church

to meet Herbert, who stood waiting for her, she felt a
choking sensation in her throat and she held her husband's hand tightly while the Reverend Charles Gardner
pronounced the young couple man and wife in front of
the fifty guests present. Her eyes rested on Allan, who
was his brother's best man, and she wondered, How long
will I have him? Her heart beat fast when she recalled the
old saying, "Your daughter is your daughter all her life,
but your son is your son until he takes a wife." However,
as she greeted friends at the wedding reception held in
the Hoovers' San Juan Hill home—since the Watsons lived
in San Francisco—she told them joyously, "Now we have
a daughter."

After the festivities, the young Hoovers went directly
to Harvard where Herbert was to take post-graduate work
in Business Administration for the next two years. His
mother depended on Allan to act as host for the many
visitors who constantly dropped by the Palo Alto home,
where wicker chairs and gay striped umbrellas were background for numerous terrace teas. He accompanied his
mother to Washington in August and he worked during
the remainder of the summer vacation as secretary in his
father's office in the Department of Commerce in Washington. He returned to Stanford in September.

That fall in Washington, Mrs. Hoover gave a colorful
reception for the international visitors from thirty-nine
countries, who came in their native costumes to attend
the peace conference of the International Council of
Women.

As the months rolled by, Mrs. Hoover saw Gilbert and
Sullivan competing with the symphony orchestras in the
entertainment world in Boston and New York. She went
eagerly to hear Arturo Toscanini, who had returned to
America after six years abroad. She watched *Ben Hur*

on the motion-picture screen, and read that this show brought in record audiences all over the country.

As the holidays approached in 1925, Lou Hoover made her annual Christmas visit to the Children's Hospital, loaded with great boxes of raisins and other dried fruit raised in her own state of California. Accompanied by Margaret Hoover, she distributed the Christmas treats personally to all the wards. The Children's Hospital was one of her chief interests all the time she lived in the capital and her annual visit as Mrs. Santa Claus was an eagerly anticipated event there.

The Hoover family spent a quiet Christmas at home in Washington.

As the new year got under way, Lou Hoover noted with anxious interest that very slow progress had been made in the District of Columbia to meet the housing and recreational needs of the thousands of young women pouring into Washington to work in government jobs. So she enthusiastically joined the Washington committee which conducted a national campaign for $700,000 to build a new YWCA at 17th and K streets.

"The money for this building should come from every state in the Union in proportion to the quota of government workers it furnishes to Washington," she declared.

But the big world suddenly narrowed down to her own family on March 18, 1926, when Lou Hoover received the exciting news that she was a grandmother. A daughter, Peggy Ann, was born to Mrs. Herbert Hoover, Jr., at Cambridge, Massachusetts, on that day, and Lou Hoover departed at once to see the baby. She looked at the newcomer with a feeling of pride and exultation as the baby's small features recalled to her mind the downy newborn look of her own children. After joyfully performing grandmotherly duties for a couple of weeks, she returned to public life.

She enjoyed especially her Girl Scout activities and was among the 200 International Scout leaders who completed a week at Irondale, Missouri, in April, just preceding the annual convention in St. Louis. She and the other leaders spent a very vigorous seven days at camp, doing their own cooking over open fires and receiving instruction in out-of-door living from forest rangers and others. Bronzed and glowing with health, this group in their immaculately tailored khaki uniforms and broad-brimmed hats lent a touch of the military, which Lou did not like, to the streets of St. Louis as they joined 400 other women from all parts of the country.

Immediately upon their arrival, Lou Hoover and the other leaders plunged into a five-day session which included separate meetings of the twelve regions of Girl Scout work in the United States. She advocated careers for women, but with home and family always to come first.

She told the convention, "I believe that even after marriage it is possible for a woman to have a career." When asked what she thought of the woman who spends all of her time taking care of her home, she replied, "I think she is lazy. The modern home is so small there is little work to do. The baby? It isn't a baby for long. There is no reason why a girl should get rusty in her profession during the five or six years she is caring for a small child."

Lou, in greeting the delegates officially, urged the great importance of camping out as a factor in the education and discipline of young people. "I have learned more from camping out than from any other influence in my life," she said. "As a child I camped with my father and later on in college I know we learned more on camping

and hiking trips for geology and biology than in the class-
room. Few episodes in my married life," continued Lou,
"have been so satisfactory as the camping trips. I have
camped in nearly every one of your countries—Australia,
Japan, Serbia, all the British dominions—and I know of
nothing that brings one so close to the really worth-while
things in a country. Let me advise you Scout leaders, do
not use camping for its own sake, however. Take your
girls out on nature-study trips or to develop some branch
of your work, such as map making. Let camping be a way
of living, not a cause of living."

The convention ended with a festival put on by 1,000
St. Louis girls in the Field House of Washington University.

When school was out that spring, Allan started on a
three-month tour of Europe and his mother saw him off.
Later in June, Lou Hoover renewed her acquaintance
with little Peggy Ann in Palo Alto, where the Junior
Hoovers went to spend the summer with the Senior
Hoovers. No grandmother ever enjoyed her new role
more. She delighted in the baby, showing her off to many
old friends that summer of 1926.

Back in Washington, with trowel and mortar in hand,
on July 15 Lou Hoover helped lay the cornerstone of the
Girl Scout Little House at its new location, 18th Street
and New York Avenue. This house was erected by the
General Federation of Women's Clubs as an exhibit of the
Better Homes in America Association and was originally
called Home, Sweet Home. It was visited by tens of thousands at its first location behind the Treasury Building
and then ceased to be an exhibit. The Scouts needed a
little house to use as an experimental center in Girl Scout
home-making activities. Mrs. Hoover arranged that the
Scouts should have it for the cost of moving. She en-

couraged the National Girl Scout organization to acquire similar little houses in many other cities.

On September 12, 1926, Lou Hoover went to New York to meet Allan, returning from his tour of Europe, and accompanied him to California where he started another year at Stanford. For hours on the train, mother and son discussed what he had seen and heard on the continent. And she told him all about baby Peggy Ann.

Back in Washington, Lou helped the Girl Scouts put on a luncheon party in November at their Little House for President and Mrs. Coolidge and several other distinguished guests. The Hoover family gathering for Christmas that year in Cambridge, Massachusetts, was child-focused and much enlivened by the presence of little Peggy Ann.

After the holidays, Lou returned to continue with her multitude of activities in women's organizations and especially in Scouting. A chief item of the Girl Scout leader's agenda in the spring of 1927 was to adopt a different uniform to replace the mannish khaki which Mrs. Hoover had never liked. A new costume of green wool with a suède belt was chosen and a feminine hat to match the new uniform replaced its stiff-brimmed, military-looking predecessor.

Early in May 1927, the dignified and conservative Daughters of the American Revolution heard Lou Hoover give a warm defense of the modern "flapper," her advanced ideas and short skirts. "I have the greatest faith and admiration for the young people of today," she said, "even for their sensible clothes, which some people seem to think are immodest." Speaking of the Girl Scout movement, she said she was amazed to find that a majority of the girls were more interested in the home-making activities than in any others.

Over the breakfast coffee on May 20, Herbert Hoover read a news item to his wife about the son of their friend the congressman from Minnesota, Charles A. Lindbergh, who was about to compete for the $25,000 prize offered to the first pilot to make a New York to Paris nonstop flight. Two days later, Lou Hoover handed her husband a newspaper with banner headlines and the story of the "Lone Eagle's" transatlantic flight from Roosevelt Field, Long Island, via Newfoundland, Ireland, and England to Paris and how he had glided his plane down on Le Bourget Field at 10:02 P.M. on May 21, after 3,600 miles in thirty-three and a half hours. Lou read about the state receptions for young Lindbergh in Paris, Brussels, and London and the innumerable decorations and trophies given him in recognition.

She was happy to help preside over the elaborate reception in Washington on June 11, when President Coolidge decorated Lindbergh for his achievement. This was the start of a long friendship with the flier. The whole country was thrilled with the modest Lone Eagle, and almost overnight America turned from tales of corruption to heroism and adventure with intense fervor.

When summer came, Lou planned a longer-than-usual stay in California to be with Allan, who was preparing for his senior year at Stanford. She also wanted to spend some time with her father in Monterey. Herbert Hoover made only one quick trip to Palo Alto that summer.

On one occasion, when Charles Henry was with them at the campus home, the conversation turned to recent publicity urging that Herbert Hoover should become a candidate for the presidency.

"Do you think Dad will run?" Allan asked his mother.

"He said we can't even think about such a thing until we know more about Mr. Coolidge's plans," replied Lou.

"But people have been talking to Dad about it for months and months," continued Allan, "so we have to think about it."

"Bert has an enviable record of service and achievement," said Charles Henry, "and I think he could be elected if he would run. It would be a fitting climax for his years of service to his country."

That afternoon Lou sat on an outdoor terrace at her hillside home and gazed down into the swimming pool below. How can we leave this place, she thought. But it would be a wonderful fulfillment for Bert, and by now I am used to living in Washington.

On August 22, 1927, Calvin Coolidge made the headlines by stating, "I do not choose to run for President in 1928."

Lou Hoover returned to Washington, resigned to the idea that it might be their home for several more years.

On November 7, 1927, she received a telegram from her sister that their father was ill in Monterey. She left immediately to be with him. When he was better, Lou held a family consultation with her father and sister and it was decided that Charles Henry should go back to Washington with her. Lou asked Jean, "Do you think that a leisurely drive across the country, camping out when possible, would help Father?"

"It might be just the thing," replied Jean.

Lou equipped a large car with the necessary provisions and engaged a Filipino to be chauffeur and handy man. Father and daughter particularly enjoyed the natural beauties of the countryside as they drove through Arizona and New Mexico at the start of the long trek.

Their conversation naturally turned to the political situation and Bert as a candidate for President.

XI

PRESIDENTIAL CAMPAIGN

AND GOOD-WILL TOUR

TO SOUTH AMERICA

•

1928

WHEN IT BECAME APPARENT that Calvin Coolidge really did not choose to run in 1928, Mrs. Hoover realized that her husband was in the battle for the Republican nomination for President of the United States. Not that it was much of a battle, for Herbert Hoover had the support of high-ranking Republicans all over the country.

Lou Hoover knew her husband could count on the personal loyalty of hordes of friends, as she remembered the legions who had worked with him while he was feeding the Belgians or in the many projects of Food Administration and Secretary of Commerce days. Now her table and drawing room became centers for much political discussion.

She was interviewed about her attitude toward suffrage and reported, "Women in politics do not seem any different than men in politics. They are both human and voters, and frankly I don't think they are very different. They are not in California where I go to the polls to vote. Here in Washington, of course, there are no local politics and voting, so I can't know about them personally in the East."

When asked how she felt when some of the feminists were battling too bitterly for the vote, she replied, "I just thought that when a majority of us really believed that we should have the vote we could sit down and talk it over with our fathers, our husbands, and our brothers. I never thought that women were downtrodden by the men before they had the vote. The main reason I wanted it was because I do think it is a good thing for laws affecting the community and the nation to be discussed over the dining table and in the library of the home."

On February 12, 1928, Herbert Hoover told his wife that he had agreed to have his name placed on the Ohio primary ballot. Shortly thereafter she read about other state primaries organizing Hoover clubs.

The wives of the men most talked about for the presidency were being discussed as the political campaign got under way. Lou Hoover was described by Frederick Collins in the *Woman's Home Companion* for April 1928 as follows:

There can be no discussion of her ability to meet the great leaders of the world, because she has met them many times in many lands. There can be no speculation as to her ability to cooperate with her husband in matters of state, because she has already done so in the greatest crises of the world's history. As a woman of the world, as an experienced observer of statesmen and statesmanship, above all as a wife, Mrs. Hoover is the ideal future mistress of what she herself describes as the most beautiful as well as the most honored home in the world.

His wife and their sons were ready to bend every effort to further the cause of Herbert Hoover's political campaign. Allan, newly graduated from Stanford, went to Kansas City on June 14 for the national Republican convention, where he unobtrusively acted as a page boy. Later, Lou Hoover listened as her handsome son told her about it.

"The big convention hall, plastered with Hoover posters, was full of wildly excited people cheering for Dad. I held my breath as the first ballot was being taken and couldn't understand the stampede and roaring ovation before the final result was announced. I thought no one was ever nominated on the first ballot. But Dad was! He received 837 votes out of 1,084 cast."

"I'm not surprised," responded his mother; "people trust him."

Allan hurried back to California to fill in the rest of the family on all the details of the convention. A few days later, Lou Hoover and her husband started by train for Palo Alto, where Bert was to be officially notified of his nomination.

During the first day of the trip, while seated at a table in the dining car, Lou had listened intently when Bert took a pencil and piece of paper out of his pocket and drew a diagram of the setup of the political organization on which he proposed to rest his hopes for the presidency. She knew he was determined to win the office for which he had been nominated not so much in anticipation of the honor at stake as in fear of failing in the trust imposed upon him by his supporters. She saw that he had a carefully conceived plan to garner votes in every city ward, country hamlet, and tiny precinct in the land. He was waging a kind of political battle new to the veteran spellbinders, but tried and proved by him in other organizational work. She knew that his name had been constantly before the people since World War I had started, and she told him, "I know you will win."

Before the end of the second day on the train, Lou received a telegram from Allan stating that her father, Charles D. Henry, aged eighty-four, had been taken ill while on a hike in the mountains and was in the hospital at Placerville. White-faced, she handed the telegram to Bert with, "Can't we do anything to speed up this train?"

With his arm across her shoulders, he promised, "We'll see if there are any stops that can be eliminated."

News of her father's death reached Lou at Omaha and they continued the sad journey to Palo Alto, where she was met by her sister, Jean Henry Large.

Lou's personal plans were modified by the passing of her father, but the presidential campaign was not to be pushed aside. Then other family events demanded her attention.

Early in the summer, she hurried home from Boston where she had greeted her first grandson. "He is Herbert Hoover the third," she told a friend at lunch, "but we call him Peter. Mr. Hoover has always been called Bert by his intimates and he nicknamed our son Pete when he was a little fellow. I think Herbert liked his father's calling him that and he takes pleasure in calling his own son Peter."

On August 17, 1928, Lou received the honorary degree of Doctor of Literature from Whittier College. As she returned to the Quaker town of her childhood in a large limousine, escorted by policemen on motorcycles, she saw streets draped with flags and she smiled and waved at the 5,000 townspeople who came out to welcome her. This place, so full of memories of her father, touched a responsive chord in her heart.

Before going to the First Friends meetinghouse, where

the degree was conferred, Lou was taken for a brief re-union with some of her girlhood friends. She was Lou Henry, the schoolgirl, again when she stepped into the lobby of the hotel where they were gathered. She walked around the room, tall, smiling, and making everyone feel recognized and important. She took men and women by their hands, looked laughingly into their faces and called them by name, even though she had not seen them in years. "It is really fun to see old friends again," and she said it as if she really meant it.

She donned the purple-and-gold gown and hood of Whittier College, joined the procession made up of faculty and the board of trustees, and marched across the street to the meetinghouse where the exercises were held, be-cause the college auditorium was not large enough to hold the audience of 2,000 people. President Walter F. Dexter, in conferring the degree, referred to Lou Hoover's humanitarian and literary work, mentioning her presi-dency of the Girl Scouts and her translation with her hus-band of *De Re Metallica*. "Your intellectual pursuits," he said, "have been broad and comprehensive . . . and have given you a place of prominence among scholars of to-day." Lou Henry Hoover was especially pleased to be recognized in the town of her early school years.

Toward the end of August, Lou Hoover, accompanied by both Herbert and Allan, made a pleasant pilgrimage back to Waterloo, Iowa, to visit her birthplace. Secretly, she was glad that the campaign press agent had planned for her to visit another childhood home.

The wife of the Republican nominee for the presidency was welcomed with enthusiastic demonstrations by her old friends and former schoolmates, who, too, had known her as Lou Henry in her early childhood days. The main street of Waterloo was gay with flags and bunting, as

crowds watched the three Hoovers arrive in an open car.
Her sons heard her described as an enthusiastic unafraid
youngster, with pigtails flying as she coasted downhill or
rode horseback.

In her own mind's eye, Lou saw the path through the
woods where she had gathered hazelnuts and trapped
rabbits with her father, and the river beyond where she
had gone fishing, and she wished she could again wear
comfortable hiking clothes with many pockets. But correct
for the time and place, Lou was dressed in a plain black
chiffon dress and wore a small black hat with a narrow
ripple brim.

Before they proceeded to the official reception, she
reviewed a group of Girl Scouts and school children on
the courthouse lawn and put her arm around the child
who presented her with a bouquet.

Presidential campaigning went into high gear that fall.
The lifetime comradeship with her husband and the merg-
ing of her life with his were illustrated again, when Lou
accompanied Herbert Hoover on a whirlwind tour of the
country. She greeted people from the train platform with
simple friendliness and chatted about the ordinary things
of life, while he educated them on the issues of the day.

At the beginning of the campaign trip, Lou had been
unwilling to make speeches or even to appear on the rear
platform, until her husband told her, "I need you there
and who else should receive all the bouquets?"

Herbert Hoover's seven major addresses of the campaign were made at Palo Alto, California; West Branch,
Iowa; Elizabethton, Tennessee; Newark, New Jersey; Boston, Massachusetts; New York City; and St. Louis, Missouri.

Lou Hoover's speeches broke all records for brevity and

graciousness. While holding an armful of flowers in Palo Alto, she said, "I enjoy campaigning because my husband makes the speeches and I receive the roses."

Chilly winds and lowering skies failed to keep her from her place beside her husband on his speaking tours. She went through days of active campaigning and came up smiling. "Am I tired? Not a bit," she said, over a huge armful of roses. "Why should I be, when all I've done is ride around and meet friendly people and receive beautiful flowers?"

It was the first presidential campaign to be broadcast by radio, and because of this Lou knew that her husband would not repeat his talks but would sit up night after night writing new speeches. He never used a ghost writer.

Lou heard her husband say in a speech in New York on October 12, 1928, "Even if government conduct of business could give us more efficiency instead of less efficiency, the fundamental objection to it would remain unaltered and unabated. It would destroy political equality, increase corruption, and stifle initiative and invention and undermine the development of leadership."

This is his fundamental belief, his wife thought proudly.

The crowd in Madison Square Garden in New York City gave them a tremendous ovation. Lou's ears were ringing with the din of 10,000 voices enthusiastically shouting, "Hoover!" Before her eyes were the laughing faces of men and women determined to prove their admiration for the Republican candidate for President by flag waving, hand clapping, stamping of feet, and throwing of confetti. Her face, untouched by cosmetics, glowed with pride and she was bright-eyed with pleasure. She smiled into the faces of the noisy gathering, evaluating the situation and noting that there seemed to be more women than men present. Maintaining an unruffled man-

ner, she thought, I mustn't let them know how weary I
am. As she boarded the special train at about 1 A.M. she
said to herself, You can't be very tired, you know, when
you are just about the proudest woman in the world.

Lou Hoover had achieved much more than to be just
a shadowy background for her husband's vigorous char-
acters. Behind her natural reserve, her own strong indi-
viduality emerged along with a deep strength of loyalty
and a joyful sharing of her husband's life.

On November 1, 1928, Mr. and Mrs. Herbert Hoover
left Washington for Palo Alto to cast their votes. Election
Day dawned warm and bright on the Stanford campus.
Lou and Bert Hoover walked to their neighborhood poll-
ing place early and then he retired to his study while
she made preparations for the friends who were to share
the evening with them. There was a great deal for her
hands to do, but nothing could still the rising excitement
in her mind. If he is elected, she mused, and he surely
will be, then we will be saying good-bye to our campus
home again.

Most of the day, the stucco house on San Juan Hill was
bulging with relatives and special guests who gathered
around the radios, listening to the broadcasts. Downtown, hundreds of Palo Alto citizens thronged the Community House outdoor theater to hear the broadcasts,
while thousands of others listened in on their home sets.
Wherever there was a radio set on public duty in the
business district, there was a crowd gathered to listen. By
evening, when the election results were becoming obvious,
there was a surge of well wishers from campus and town
filling all the terraces and completely surrounding the
Hoover house.

"He is bound to make it now," exulted Allan, as he gave
Herbert a brotherly slap on the back to acknowledge a

late official report brought in by a state trooper from the national hookup in the garage. Lou Hoover was radiant when Allan told her, "The final tally shows that Dad carried 40 of the 48 states, was elected with 444 electoral votes out of a possible 531, and polled 21½ million popular votes. And that is better than anyone else ever did before in a presidential election!"

Lou went in search of Bert and slipping her hand into his said quietly, "I knew you could do it."

Crowds followed John Philip Sousa and his band up the hill from the university, where they had been giving a concert. The Hoovers went out on the second-level terrace above the front door and were serenaded. As they lined up, Herbert stood close to Peggy, who held baby Peter in her arms. Next came Lou with an excited Peggy Ann, then Bert, the successful candidate, with a pleased smile on his face, and finally Allan.

The happy crowd cheered and sang and were loath to disperse until Mrs. Hoover declared, finally, "We must take the children inside now."

During the four months between election and inauguration, Lou Hoover and Allan accompanied the President-elect on an unofficial diplomatic journey to Latin America.

"Your father has real optimism and courage to undertake a good-will tour of South America in six weeks' time," she told Allan, "but he feels we should try to advance international cordiality between the Americas. He has had a good deal of experience in various mines there and knows how the people of South America feel."

A diplomatic staff and many representatives of the press were included in the group, partly to evidence interest in Central and South America and partly to educate the North American people through the newspaper accounts sent home. Lou Hoover, who could speak a good deal of Spanish, was a valuable member of the team.

President Coolidge assigned the battleship *Maryland* to take the party south and later arranged for the *Utah* to meet them in Montevideo for the return trip. On shipboard, Lou Hoover and Allan relaxed while the President-elect assembled his administrative staff and spent much time formulating major policies for the next four years.

He told the newsmen, "We expect no startling agreements and no historic understandings, but instead, friendly face-to-face talks between the heads of the Latin-American countries and ourselves."

After a week at sea, the good-will tourists made their first calls at Ampala, Honduras, and at La Union, San Salvador. The next was in San José, Costa Rica, on November 29. President Gonzales Viquez and his official family met them and explained that the honor guard would be school children because their country had virtually no army. This delighted Mrs. Hoover.

She thought that the outstanding event of their visit to Nicaragua was that both President Díaz and President-elect Moncada, leaders of different political factions, joined forces to meet Herbert Hoover and agreed with him that obstructionist tactics would be abandoned.

The first stop in South America was at Guayaquil, Ecuador. President Ayora of Ecuador welcomed the good-will tourists and was entertained aboard the USS *Maryland* before it weighed anchor for the next leg of the journey southward.

Lou was especially interested in the brilliant function held on the afterdeck of the *Maryland* anchored off Antofagasta, Chile, where her husband had once investigated the world's largest copper mines for the Guggenheim family.

A day or two later, the *Maryland* landed the tourists at Callao, the port of Valparaiso, Chile, and then returned to the United States. The party traveled in automobiles from Callao to Lima, Peru. While her husband dined with President Leguia and other public officials, Lou Hoover enjoyed a tour of the city and a formal luncheon replete with entertainment by native dancers on the stage of the banquet hall.

She was touched by the unusual honor accorded them in Santiago when the President of Chile, himself, came to the railroad station to meet them in the capital city. They rode through five miles of splendid avenues in a gold-decorated carriage of state and saw people throwing flowers and smiling, crowding the sidewalks, balconies, and roofs.

The Hoover party had an unforgettable journey over the Andes. Starting with a breath-taking, narrow-gauge, ladderlike climb up the steep western slopes of Chile's Andes, they spent four days on the trans-Andean railway, a 700-mile trip to reach Buenos Aires. They were accompanied by a delegation of Chilean government officials, financial and engineering experts to the borderline of the summit of the Andes and from there on by a similar delegation of Argentinians.

At Mendoza, they changed from the small Chilean train to a big, comfortable one that took them to the Argentina seaport.

On December 15, a small anti-American demonstration in Buenos Aires gave Lou some concern, but Mayor José Cantilo quickly suppressed it and the group from the United States was feted, went sight-seeing through the streets of the capital, and appeared at several receptions. Mrs. Hoover accompanied her husband when he was taken to the city hall to receive a gold medal, the gift of the municipality, and she felt that they were being shown every mark of friendliness and respect by the vast majority of the residents of the city.

At Montevideo, they boarded the USS *Utah* for the journey up the east coast of South America and back to the United States. The *Utah* entered the harbor at Rio de Janeiro about noon on December 21, to the most spectacular welcome of the whole good-will tour, complete with gala greetings of welcome. Lou became acutely aware that she was the wife of the President-elect of the United States of America. The front pages of the newspapers were devoted largely to photographs of the Hoover family, the house where Herbert Hoover was born, and the White House, their next residence.

On December 22, Lou Hoover, accompanied by Allan, spent two hours shopping in stores on Avenida Rio Blanca. As they surveyed the white linen suits and dresses, white hats and white shoes, Allan said, "Looks like a white Christmas here with no snow."

"We will have Christmas aboard the *Utah*," replied Lou, "so we must make some decorations." They purchased a small artificial tree, two dozen red candles and some tinsel to decorate the dining salon of the battleship.

Installed in the admiral's quarters on the *Utah*, vacated for her, Lou settled down to the home-bound routine. By now the Hoovers were on terms of pleasant and easy intimacy with the officers, the crew, and the newspaper correspondents aboard the battleship and there was a family air about it. Every afternoon Mrs. Hoover entertained at tea on deck, while her husband worked at laying the foundations of his new administration. His books on South America were shared with his wife, naturally, and as she read more and more about their neighbors to the south and recalled significant events of the trip, she devoutly hoped and believed that this first good-will tour had built bridges of understanding between North and South America and had cemented friendships among their people.

After the strenuous trip to South America, Lou and Bert Hoover had a holiday at Miami Beach at the J. C. Penney estate on Belle Isle, a jewel in the emerald waters of Biscayne Bay, which provided them with an ideal spot for fishing. During the brief stay in Florida, they were showered with invitations to social functions of various sorts, but for the most part they derived their enjoyment by entertaining close friends informally at their Belle Isle home, cruising, motoring, and fishing. They were seldom seen in public except when attending Friends' meeting. Lou thought wistfully, this is the end of our private life for four years, so we should make the most of it. Nevertheless, noting how much the weeks in Florida had helped her husband to relax, she boarded the special train for Washington, D.C., on February 18, still a little ruefully, but with pleasant expectations for the new life awaiting them.

The very day she returned to Washington, Lou Hoover began her usual pattern of entertaining. She gave a luncheon for Colonel Charles Lindbergh and his fiancée, Anne Morrow, daughter of the Hoovers' good friend, Dwight Morrow, United States Ambassador to Mexico.

Her social life was complicated and although she accepted protocol, she was sensitive as always to personal relationships and was distressed when a traditional dinner conflicted with an evening planned by old friends.

Seven hundred people, who had worked with the Hoovers in Belgium or in Food Administration projects, met at the Wardman Park Hotel on March 3 for a gala dinner in their honor. It was planned to be the last act as private citizens for the honor guests. Old friends clasped hands, reminisced, and shed tears for comrades passed on, while they awaited "the Chief."

Then the big disappointment was announced; neither Mr. nor Mrs. Hoover could be present because of the protocol that the outgoing President should entertain the President-elect for dinner and conduct him over the White House on the eve of inauguration. To offset the disappointment, however, Lou Hoover had sent written invitations to be handed to each one attending the dinner for a reception at the White House immediately after the inaugural parade.

XII

FIRST LADY OF THE LAND

•

1929

THE MORNING OF March 4, 1929, dawned bleak and gray. Lou Hoover had hoped that the sky would clear for the inauguration, but that morning she saw, instead, heavy storm clouds.

The day began early for her, with a house full of happy relatives and with messages, letters, and flowers pouring in every minute. One of the gifts that interested her most, presented by Representative Florence Kahn, congresswoman of San Francisco, was a beautiful bouquet of orchids from the women of California. As Lou Hoover glanced out of the windows of her beloved S Street house, that she was leaving for at least four years, she saw people already gathering to watch the proceedings.

The Hoover family party was augmented by Lou's sister, Mrs. Jean Large, with her daughter Janet and William Henry, her uncle. Herbert, with Peggy and Peggy Ann, came from their new home in Los Angeles, where the young father was employed. A merry little child, Peggy Ann, aged four, attached herself to her uncle Allan, with whom she was a prime favorite. When arrayed for the trip to the Capitol, her proud grandmother thought that Peggy Ann was the picture of joyous childhood in a coat of blue cloth with a fur collar and tiny cuffs of fur. Baby brother Peter, being too young to witness the ceremony, was left in Los Angeles with his maternal grandmother.

Herbert Hoover picked up President Coolidge at the White House and rode to the Capitol with him. Their wives followed in a separate car.

On arriving at the Capitol building, the presidential party started for the inauguration place. Lou Hoover, walking with Grace Coolidge, saw that the grandstands erected outside the East Portico of the Capitol were jammed with 100,000 people watching the notables arriving to fill the folding chairs. The clouds grew more dense and rain began to fall. With a sigh of relief, Lou observed that the platform in front of the grandstands where President-elect Hoover was to take his oath of office had a canvas cover. There were amplifiers, a large copy of the Food Administration seal, red roses on the balustrade, everywhere American flags and, of course, umbrellas of every color, shape, and kind.

Mrs. Coolidge and Mrs. Hoover were temporarily separated from their official escort. As they struggled to get through the throng of people, diplomats, members of the House and Senate, and the justices of the Supreme Court in their robes of office, arrived and were seated. Lou saw Bert and Mr. Coolidge conducted to their places and then there was a pause as they looked anxiously around for their wives.

"Will we ever be able to force our way through this crowd?" Lou Hoover asked anxiously, but Grace Coolidge reassured her as the aides quickly assisted them, quite out of breath, to their places at the back of the platform.

The two women sank gratefully into their seats just in time to see Senator Curtis take his oath of office as vice President. Then, deeply moved, Lou Hoover watched the impressive Chief Justice Howard Taft rise to administer the presidential oath to her husband, whose interests she had vitally shared, as well as his home.

Sitting on a hard chair in the drizzle, she experienced one of the greatest moments of her life. How wisely I chose, she thought, when I married that earnest, devoted young man who worked his way through Stanford.

The rain came pelting down while Lou heard Bert promise, "I solemnly swear to faithfully execute the office of President of the United States and will to the best of my ability preserve, protect, and defend the Constitution."

When he became the thirty-first President of the United States, she saw her early faith in Bert fulfilled more completely than even she could have expected. She took her eyes from her husband only to glance at the thousands of loyal citizens standing in the cold downpour watching this important ceremony.

The new President had to brush the rain from his eyes as he began his speech. The wind blew in gusts and it grew so cold and miserable that hundreds were forced to leave their seats reluctantly, to find shelter. As Lou Hoover sat there, a quiet, dignified figure in a black broadtail coat and plum-colored hat and dress, she hoped that the crowd of women in small bright hats huddling under their umbrellas would have faith in her as First Lady of the land.

The inaugural parade was held in spite of the stormy weather. Lou Hoover joined the rest of her family on the balcony of the White House and with evident great pleasure watched the intrepid marchers pass by in the rain. "There are Virginia's celebrated Richmond troops," she exclaimed. "What a striking picture they make in their blue uniforms and white cockades against the dull gray sky." Governors and other important people rode in closed cars. Lou's enthusiasm did not dampen, and she frequently called attention to interesting groups which were passing by.

"I hope the rain won't interfere with the fireworks tonight," observed Allan, "but anyway it won't spoil the dancing at the Auditorium Ball afterward."

While this was going on in Washington, three thousand miles across the country throngs of people on the Pacific coast were listening in on the radio to hear the voice of Herbert Hoover pronouncing the solemn oath of office which made him President of the United States.

As Lou Hoover changed her dress for the reception at the White House, which was to follow the parade, she listened to the broadcast of a special program from Stanford and was thrilled to learn that her friends at home were also participating in Bert's big day. She was affected by a sudden wave of keen emotion as she heard the voices of the student choir, directed by Warren D. Allen, organist, in the Memorial church, sing "Hail, Stanford, Hail," the hymn of their Alma Mater.

An hour later, Lou Hoover stood beside her husband in the Blue Room and gave cordial greetings to hundreds of reception guests. With this first entertaining, Lou introduced a much more liberal form of hospitality than had prevailed in the previous administration. At this first reception, she served tea in the dining room with a great variety of goodies and generous supplies of everything.

March 5 was a pleasantly busy first day at the White House for Lou, who went about her business of setting the new home in order with the same cheerful efficiency with which she had made homes for her family at one time or another in the far corners of the world. She had never suspected then that the White House would be one of those homes. A wide variety of activities, ranging from a large reception for the Republican National Committee to the homely pleasure of an hour's romp with her small granddaughter Peggy Ann, who would soon return to California, claimed her attention.

When she moved into the White House, Lou Hoover was sensitive to the historical significance of its many rooms and halls. After consultation with her husband, she reestablished the President's study in the room which had been used for that purpose by all the presidents from Adams to McKinley, but was changed into a bedroom by the Theodore Roosevelts. Abraham Lincoln had signed the Emancipation Proclamation there and Lou Hoover, after studying a painting which depicted the event, discovered some of the original furniture stored away in the attic. She refurbished the study and restored much of the original furniture. The Hoovers' much-traveled steel engraving of Lincoln and his Cabinet found still another resting place—a most appropriate one—in Bert's new study.

Loving history as much as she did, it was natural that Lou should be delighted to discover in the Monroe law office in Fredericksburg, Virginia, many pieces of the old French furniture acquired by President Monroe after the British burned the White House in 1812. She had some of these pieces copied at her own expense and placed in the Rose Drawing Room on the second floor. Later she left them as her gift to the White House.

Mrs. Hoover always wanted people to be comfortable, and she rearranged the White House to make it as homelike as possible—without, however, destroying its authentic character. She bought fifty comfortable chairs which

could be used for occasional moving pictures or for conferences held at the east end of the long second-story
hall. She added enough bookcases along the sides of this
hall to take proper care of myriads of books. At the west
end of the hall she put plants and a few canaries in cages.

She also had a number of other chairs purchased for
the East Room, the huge formal reception hall on the
first floor. Before this time, there were only upholstered
benches placed around the wall to seat the guests for the
musicals held there after state dinners. She, personally,
bought lovely green taffeta curtains for the Oval Room
on the second floor. Following those dinners which were
not state ones, the ladies went to this room while the men
gathered in the President's study.

But Lou Hoover was concerned with more than her
own family's living quarters and the public rooms. She
provided comfortable furniture in which White House
workers could rest, and a cool place for them to sleep.
In no time she knew all about the employees, their families and their ambitions. She kept on all the servants
previously employed, many of whom had served in the
White House for years. The head cook confessed to her
that she had voted for Alfred Smith and expected to lose
her job. But she stayed on and became a loyal friend when
the new First Lady assured her, "I am not concerned
with your political preferences but with your superlative
cooking."

Lou turned over the detailed planning for the children's
annual Easter egg rolling on the White House lawn to
her personal secretary, Miss Mildred Hall. On Monday,
April 1, 1929, 20,000 children appeared with their little
baskets for holding the gayly colored eggs, and had a
wonderful time despite overcast skies and soggy under-
footing. Mrs. Hoover had invited her former neighbors on

S Street to be special guests, but no adult was admitted unless accompanied by a child. The children from S Street were permitted to occupy the South Portico of the White House, along with the children of members of the Cabinet and the Diplomatic Corps. Some of them appeared decidedly impatient under this restraint and strongly indicated that they would much prefer to be down on the lawn hunting eggs than standing with the favored few on the portico.

Police Sergeant Clarence Dalrymple, who admitted the guests at the East Gate, said that if any nationality on earth was not represented, he did not know which it was. Lou joined the merrymakers several times during the day and watched the children scampering up and down the lawn, gleefully rolling their multicolored eggs down the slope and putting on impromptu races of all kinds. Miss Hall added new features to the party. She arranged with Neighborhood House for the children to have a Maypole dance. The Girl Scouts did folk dancing, accompanied by the Marine Band, and the Boy Scouts were commissioned to find lost children. Several small boys did a rushing business outside the gates, selling their own "escort" services to adults who wanted to see the new First Lady in action.

Mrs. Hoover was constantly in the public eye and constantly involved in social affairs, but she managed to live her own life. "Be yourself," was her motto, and she lived up to it. She met adequately all the formal demands made upon the mistress of the White House, but on unofficial occasions she exercised the right to be herself and went her own informal way. She continued to drive her own car around Washington and to take picnic lunches to enjoy along the road when she went on trips. Even in dress, she mastered the difficult art of being her individual self while conforming to the demands of current fashion. She dressed simply and preferred a tailored dress for daytime and a stately gown for evening.

With the heat of a Washington summer upon them, Lou Hoover was concerned that her husband was working too hard. She was distressed because he was under such pressure that he decided he could not take any vacation. As they walked together in the garden one evening discussing the matter, they came upon a small furry object, desperately frightened and trying to hide in the shrubbery. Lou helped catch the little possum and put him in a cage on the lawn. He was duly christened "Billy" and adopted as a White House mascot. Catching "Billy" made Lou long to walk in the woods again and to get away from the city.

"Why don't we find a little house in the mountains for a weekend retreat, and have a little privacy?" she asked. "Then you would be close enough always to be available in case of an emergency."

"It is a good idea," Bert agreed, "and we will start looking for the right place immediately."

He commissioned Lawrence Richy, a White House secretary, and Marine Major Earl Long to begin the hunt. They discovered 1,500 acres in an ideal location near the headwaters of the Rapidan River in the Blue Ridge Mountains. It was at an elevation of 2,500 feet, yet only one hundred miles from Washington.

Lou Hoover planned the building of a summer camp there. She designed and oversaw the construction of several log cabins clustered around the main building with its big living room and open fireplace. The cabins provided accommodations for about fifteen guests. A few dams were built along the river canyon and the stream was stocked with trout. The camp was put to use before

it was completely finished. The first guests slept in tents.
Weekends found Lou Hoover a gracious camp hostess
in a setting of trees and streams. With her feet shod in
flat-heeled walking shoes, she hiked along the mountain
trails, across steppingstones and fallen logs, leading the
way and talking to her guests of many things. She often
covered eight or ten miles in a day, carrying a basket to
bring back woodsy plants for the "memory garden" at
the Girl Scouts' Little House in Washington.

On many of the Rapidan weekends Lou Hoover was
able to do some of her official entertaining in the delight-
fully informal setting of the camp, much appreciated by
the guests. She often refused to observe the long-standing
role that the wife of the President must be accompanied
by a chauffeur and Secret Service men, and drove her own
car to and from the Blue Ridge camp.

Among the official guests who enjoyed a weekend at the
camp were, in early October 1929, Prime Minister Ramsay
MacDonald and his daughter Ishbel. Lou Hoover enjoyed talking with this singularly simple and vital English-
man and the daughter, a nineteen-year-old who had all
the poise of a woman of the world, while they preceded
the President to the camp.

As was her custom with strangers, during the hundred-
mile drive to Camp Rapidan, Mrs. Hoover pointed out the
historic spots along the way: Arlington, which once belonged to George Washington and later became the home
of Robert E. Lee; Fairfax, named for the famous British
family; and Manassas, where the first major battle of the
Civil War took place. The highway ascended from the
valley into the mountains through impressively beautiful
country. As they emerged from a second horseshoe bend
in the road, Mrs. Hoover naturally pointed out to the

MacDonalds the river which had been named for a British queen. It was once called the Rapid Anne.

She also explained to the Prime Minister how the beautiful mountain scenery before them had brought about the proposal for the creation of Shenandoah National Park.

"The people who live in these mountains," she told Ishbel, "are Americans of the old colonial stock. They are long, rangy, hospitable, religious, and courageous. They have not been in the mainstream of education. We hope to start a school for the children in this sparsely settled region."

Back in Washington on Monday, there were ceremonies at the Capitol and state functions at the White House and at the British Embassy for the distinguished visitors. The Hoovers planned a state dinner for them, with a few tea parties thrown in for good measure.

Much was printed about Lou Hoover and her parties on the women's pages of the newspapers at that time. Washington had known the new First Lady for ten years, first as the wife of the Food Administrator during World War I, then for seven years as the wife of the Secretary of Commerce.

One article described her qualifications to be First Lady. It was noted that she was a grandmother but loved to ride horses; a college woman, coauthor of a technical book, but made her home and her family her career. She attended to the infinite duties that fell to the White House hostess, yet belonged to the Girl Scouts and went on camping trips with them. She often greeted as many as 200 guests for tea and could smile without effort at the last departing one.

The Washington *Post* described Lou Hoover as "a very handsome woman who looks younger than her years except for prematurely gray hair, which she wears coronet fashion around her head, and holds her slender body in an attitude of erect alertness. She moves quickly and talks quickly and has the unconscious grace of movement of an athlete and out-of-doors woman.

"Even though fond of the out-of-doors, Mrs. Hoover has many domestic traits, including a fondness for knitting, begun during World War I, when knitting was an art practiced constantly by her for the boys overseas. Now some of her knitting skill is devoted to the interests of her grandchildren.

"The woman in the White House has the point of view of an experienced, widely-traveled woman of the world. She has a healthy, sane grasp of world needs as seen through the eyes of an idealist and social-service worker."

As Thanksgiving approached, Lou Hoover longed to be out of the public eye and to have a family gathering for the holiday. Herbert and his family were in Pasadena, California, and could not make the trip. But Allan, who was registered for a two-year course at the Harvard School of Business Administration, came to Washington to be with his parents. On Thanksgiving morning, Lou and Herbert Hoover attended church services and then went for a ride into the country. The remainder of the holiday was celebrated in the White House with a quiet family dinner, early enough in the afternoon for Allan to catch the train back to Boston.

On the way to the station, Lou Hoover confided to her son that she was upset and worried because she had detected some unfriendly attitudes toward his father. "You wouldn't believe it," she said, "but some people are actually blaming him for the Wall Street crash."

Lou was disturbed again on December 7 when the Washington *Herald* devoted pages of space to denouncing the Kellogg Peace Pact, and President Hoover and the administration for upholding it. She remembered the pleasant relationship with Secretary of State Frank B. Kellogg during their London days, and believed with her husband in the principle of renunciation of war as a national policy. For the next several days, she read numerous newspaper accounts of the pros and cons of American participation in the League of Nations' World Court and was particularly offended by one editorial jab at the President for "steering the ship of state on to the rocks of internationalism."

Before Christmas, the First Lady had busy days buying and distributing gifts. She visited the Salvation Army camp, the Walter Reed Hospital, and several homes for shut-ins. She distributed toys, candy, fruit, and nuts to children at the Central Union Mission's Kiddie Bag party at the Fox Theater on December 23. After wading through the slush into the building, she tried in vain to bring order to a Christmas party of 1,400 wildly excited children. Anyway, she had a good time and so did the children. The First Lady agreed they were all "good children" and that Santa Claus would not pass by a single one of them. "Get the right children lined up for the right bags," she directed laughingly. "And I wish everyone a Merry Christmas and the same to all the children who could not be here today."

The White House was beautiful with Christmas greens arranged under the skilled supervision of the First Lady. To the right and left of the front entrance stood a tree aglow with lights, and in every window a holly wreath was hung. Among the many gifts to arrive was a fifty-pound fruitcake, baked and sent from friends in California. It was decorated with a bear and an American flag. Children would love seeing this, thought Lou.

No Hoover grandchildren were available for the 1929 holidays in Washington, since Herbert and his family were still in California. So Mrs. Hoover "adopted" eight children belonging to the White House staff and invited them with their parents for a Christmas Eve party. There were lively games and music by the Marine Band and the big fruitcake decorated with the bear for refreshments. The fun was interrupted by the clang of fire trucks and sirens close by. With her usual calm in handling emergencies, Lou Hoover directed the band to continue playing while she investigated. When she returned she called the children around her and explained in a quiet way that when their fathers left the party, they had to do so because their offices were on fire. She asked the children if they would like to go up to the second story and see the smoke. Eight pairs of scampering feet took the unfrightened children to a good vantage point to watch the fire.

Children were always a joy to Lou Hoover, no matter in what situation she encountered them. While fifty of the girls and boys from the Episcopal Home for Children watched, she turned the first shovelful of dirt at the ground-breaking exercises for their new home at Nebraska and Utah avenues. The First Lady was greeted by the youngsters with enthusiastic flag waving. Little Dorothy Robey presented her with a bouquet of pink roses while the children sang a song for her. Lou accepted the roses and then held Dorothy's flag for her so the little girl could turn over a shovelful of dirt. Then she gave the shovel to small George Smith, so that he might assist on behalf of the boys in the home.

Lou Hoover spoke directly to the children, saying, "You and I will always remember this day and when the new home is built I shall come to see you in it." Mindful of the cold weather, she added, "It's cold, children, turn up your collars, just like this," and she turned up the collar of her own coat high above her ears. Instantly fifty little collars went up above fifty youthful faces.

All children are appealing, Lou thought, whether they are orphans or your own grandchildren.

XIII

THE WHITE HOUSE DURING
1930-1931

As THE FIRST LADY of the land, Lou Hoover had to maintain many social precedents and she was very conscientious about her official entertaining, but introduced some innovations as well. Many receptions were scheduled for specific groups in the course of each year. The largest one, by far, was held on January 1, at the White House and was open to the public.

On New Year's Day 1930, a long line of people waited from midnight to get in and shake hands with the Hoovers, even though the official time of starting the reception was 11 A.M. By nine o'clock, Mrs. Hoover was worried.

"We can't keep all those people waiting another two hours," she told her husband. So the door was opened and the crowds surged inside, in orderly fashion, all intent upon greeting the first family. Before the day was over, 9,000 people had gone through the reception line.

Lou Hoover found this a very exhausting experience, even though the President sent her away for a little rest several times during the day. Discussing the affair afterward, he said, "We should abolish all big receptions, because they put too much physical strain on you."

"They are just as much strain for you, too," replied his wife, "but I know that thousands of people will be disappointed if they can't visit the White House and meet the President. So I'm afraid that the New Year's reception is one of the precedents we must follow while we are in the official residence."

Tradition assumed that there would be conventional diplomatic receptions, cabinet dinners, receptions for members of the Senate and House of Representatives, for army and navy officials, and many others. From past experience, Lou Hoover knew that these functions were sometimes stiff and formal, so she planned ahead meticulously for each event.

"For those arduous entertaining duties," she explained to a visitor from Palo Alto, "I depend upon my efficient secretaries, Miss Mildred Hall, Mrs. Frederic Butler, and Miss Doris Goss. I much prefer to guide the social program with the aid of these young women to keep the receptions from being too stiff. Guests under their direction mingle at will in the drawing room instead of gazing at grandeur from a distance. Cabinet members no longer sit like puppets in a row but are skillfully scattered through the crowd." And she added, "We try to make them comfortable."

At afternoon receptions, instead of being obliged to balance their teacups on their knees, guests found a number of small tables at hand on which to rest them. Cords, which once divided special guests and ordinary guests at the public receptions, were taken down by order of the First Lady so that a congressman's secretary could mingle freely with cabinet officers and diplomats under the new regime. This was a break with the tradition of former White House mistresses.

While giving a round of teas for the wives of congressmen, on June 12, 1930, Mrs. Hoover invited Mrs. Oscar De Priest, wife of the Negro representative from Chicago, along with the others. It never occurred to her to exclude anyone on the list, but she always tried to make her guests comfortable. For this reason, she had arranged the teas on two different days, including Mrs. De Priest with a group of women sounded out in advance as to their prejudices.

The tea party went off well and the tactful hostess was pleased. But at breakfast the next day she saw her name in the headlines. The color drained out of her face.

"Look, Bert!" she cried, pointing them out. "It says 'Mrs. Hoover Defiles the White House.' They can't mean it. Oh, it just can't be true!"

"Well, I guess that is the way lots of the Southerners feel about Negroes," he replied, his voice tense.

This tea party caused a great commotion in Washington and particularly in the South, where there were speeches and editorials about Mrs. Hoover "defiling the White House." On June 13, the Texas legislature passed a resolution denouncing her for entertaining Mrs. De Priest. Newspaper stories ran on for days and the issue just would not die.

Editorials rebuking the First Lady appeared in the Houston, Texas, *Chronicle;* the Austin, Texas, *Times;* the Montgomery, Alabama, *Advertiser;* the Memphis, Tennessee, *Commercial Appeal;* and the Jackson, Mississippi, *Daily News.* In general, the editorials from the North were as laudatory as the ones from the South were censorious. She was complimented for her stand and praised by editors of the Washington *Post, The New York Times,* the Boston *Journal*, the New York *World*, the Chicago *Daily Tribune*, the Cleveland *Gazette*, the Boston *Evening Transcript*, and the Topeka *Plain Dealer.*

Lou Hoover was still greatly upset over the Texas legislature resolution condemning her, when her husband comforted her by saying, "This issue is teeming with the same intolerance shown by both Republicans and Democrats who would have none of Al Smith because he is Catholic."

Lou winced as she read one editorial from the Mobile, Alabama, *Press* stating

> Mrs. Herbert Hoover offered to the South and to the nation an arrogant insult yesterday when she entertained a Negro woman at a White House tea. She has harmed Mr. Hoover to a serious extent. Social admixture of the Negro and the white is sought by neither race. The Negro is entitled to a social life, but that the two races should intermingle at afternoon teas or other functions is inadmissible.

But the next paper she picked up, from Bristol, Virginia, helped bolster her courage when she read an editorial that started

> The President of the United States is President of all the people, white, black, red, or yellow. The First Lady entertained a Negro at the White House as a courtesy from one branch of government to another. Mrs. Hoover is internationally minded. Politically she put into practice the brotherhood of man and religiously the fatherhood of God, even if the individual is an image carved in ebony.

Although she was very sensitive and public criticism deeply wounded her, Mrs. Hoover maintained an imperturbable outward bearing. Inwardly, she was greatly dis-

tressed and lost sleep over this barrage, but she was determined to continue doing what she thought was right.
The next week she again felt her husband's support when
he invited a Negro, Dr. Moton of Tuskegee, to the White
House for lunch. This whole episode resulted in the First
Lady becoming a little more reserved in her manner toward reporters, and some people accused her of being
cold, but she kept on with her entertaining.

Democracy surrendered socially to royalty and social
history was inscribed at a state dinner when a reigning
monarch was seated on the right of the President. Following the customs of a far older world, their majesties King
Prajadhipok and Queen Rambai Barni of Siam (now Thai-
land) were entertained with the Queen on the President's
left and the First Lady on the King's right.

The dinner came at the end of a strenuous day for the
five-foot tall, absolute monarch of Siam, but he beamed
with undiminished enthusiasm at the other fifty-eight
guests. Speaking English fluently and idiomatically, both
of the Siamese sovereigns chatted animatedly throughout
the meal. Small, slim, and ravishingly pretty, with olive
skin and smooth black hair, Queen Rambai Barni was an
exquisite picture in a golden gown of heavy brocade.
After coffee had been served, one hundred additional
guests came in for an hour of music.

The First Lady and the Queen planned a trip to Mt.
Vernon to visit the home of George Washington for the
next day, while the King received an honorary degree of
Doctor of Laws from George Washington University.
Their hostess thoroughly enjoyed this diminutive couple
and tried to make their American visit a most pleasant one
for them.

During that summer of 1930 there were many other
official guests to be entertained. In rapid succession, Mrs.

Hoover was hostess to President-elect Enrique Olaya of Colombia and Dr. Julio Prentes, President-elect of Brazil. She remembered the cordial receptions she had received in South America during her recent tour and took pleasure in making the arrangements for state dinners where the visiting rulers received high honors.

Nevertheless, she still preferred to entertain informally and enjoyed giving garden parties. She did special planning for a colorful fete for disabled war veterans, held on the south grounds of the White House on July 27. She and the President welcomed several hundred disabled World War veterans, as well as a group from the Spanish and Civil wars. Lou remembered acutely her wartime days in Europe as she said a few special words of greeting to each veteran. The line filed past while the Marine Band played patriotic airs. Many of the men were on crutches or in wheel chairs attended by nurses. The delicious sandwiches, ice cream, and punch disappeared so rapidly that fresh supplies had to be ordered.

Billy, the possum, was the center of much interest and served to relax the stiffness of some of the visitors. Lou Hoover took one group of them over to see Billy, and explained, "He is housed in a cage in the lawn once occupied by Rebecca, former President Coolidge's famous raccoon. Billy just wandered into the White House grounds several weeks ago and likes his board and room here."

A most enjoyable aspect of Mrs. Hoover's new role was entertaining at the White House people of outstanding achievement, such as Helen Keller, deaf, dumb, and blind, whose mastery of those handicaps made her one of the marvels of her age. Both the First Lady and the President were unusually attentive to the eager, serene-faced guest. Miss Keller had just broadcast over a nationwide radio network from a world conference on Work for the Blind, in a voice that might have been stilled forever, or at least inarticulate, had it not been for the inspiring courage of this gallant woman and the devotion of her teachers.

"The significance of this conference is world cooperation, something, Mr. President, you have always stood for," she said simply.

Afterward, Lou Hoover told Allan, "At luncheon I was amazed that Miss Keller seemed aware of everything that went on during her visit. Her sensitive fingers received from the lips or hands of her teacher, Mrs. Anne Sullivan Macy, or her secretary, Miss Polly Thompson, the comments of her hosts and tapped back messages in addition to her vocal expressions of delight in her surroundings."

Later in August Mrs. Hoover happily planned a small, intimate luncheon for Colonel and Mrs. Charles Lindbergh, when they flew from New York for the aviator to receive from the President a Special Medal of Honor, at presentation ceremonies on the south lawn of the White House. This medal was conferred on the colonel by congress to mark the nation's appreciation for his many contributions to the advancement of aviation. Following the ceremony, Lou Hoover and Allan motored with the Lindberghs to Camp Rapidan, where a weekend conference on aviation was scheduled for military leaders. Mrs. Hoover explained that the President would be detained in Washington until he could complete some arrangements for his extensive drought-relief program. She revealed how worried he was about the economic consequences of the long drought on the farmers' incomes, and how he was distressed to read about the number of suicides in farm families who had all their savings swept away. She added that he was studying the causes of the disaster as well as instituting relief measures. This brought a sympathetic response from Anne Lindbergh.

Lou Hoover pointed out to Anne the many changes that were still being made at the camp to allow for weekend conferences, such as the one on aviation, to be held there. Last year's tents had been turned into cottages. "Roughing it in perfect comfort," was Allan's description of the facilities as they evolved. Each cottage had a bedroom, living room, fireplace, bath, and rustic porch. There was the "town hall," a large L-shaped building—one room with two huge stone fireplaces equipped with tables, chairs, bookcases, benches, and desks, all built by the Marine camp guards in their spare time. This general gathering place provided all kinds of games, puzzles, books, and magazines. Meals were served sometimes in the "mess hall" and sometimes on tables set out under the trees beside the river. The rough rock-hewn trails about the camp had been smoothed out into winding paths, and the permanent camp became an amazing mixture of picturesque idealism and common sense—and it breathed supreme serenity.

After an early breakfast the next morning, Lou Hoover and Anne Lindbergh, dressed in khaki, rode horseback on the secluded mountain heights of Camp Rapidan, enjoying the magic beauty of late summer out-of-doors. Lou told her guest, "I, personally, test all the new horses sent up to Rapidan camp to see if they are sure-footed enough to offer to my guests. When riding at Rapidan, my own favorite is this strong bay horse. The steep, rocky, twisting, Blue Ridge trails require a very different type of mount from the kind used in a city park."

Between weekends, the First Lady was a striking figure on the Washington bridle paths. Sitting easily on her handsome gray horse, she was again in the out-of-doors

world that she loved, and she relaxed to the movement
of her gaited mount.

Then one evening, Lou Hoover slipped on a rug in
her living room and suffered a painfully wrenched back
as she fell. Confined to her rooms for three weeks by Dr.
Joel Boone, White House physician, she was finally allowed to get about in a wheel chair to receive visitors.
Despite her discomfort, she continued to act as a cheerful hostess and dispense hospitality to selected groups,
including a party of visiting Japanese girls and a delegation of Girl Scouts, who were thrilled at being received
in the First Lady's private quarters.

When not receiving visitors, Lou Hoover passed the
time reading, knitting, and keeping up with her voluminous correspondence. She wrote many personal letters on
her own typewriter during the period of her inactivity.

Because of unseasonal weather and her own incapacity,
Mrs. Hoover had to give up several weekends at Rapidan,
but she projected her thoughts to the dream camp she
had created by conferring on plans for the rock garden
which she wanted to have constructed there.

As soon as springtime weather permitted, she sought
seclusion at Rapidan to convalesce from the injury to
her back. Here she helped add finishing touches to a
school for the poor mountain children who lived in a sub-
culture of their own, ignorant of many of the ordinary
things of the civilized world. During the preceding year,
Lou Hoover had explored the Blue Ridge Mountains near
Camp Rapidan on horseback and had called upon her
neighbors in their mud-chinked log cabins. On dismount-
ing, she was promptly surrounded by ragged, illiterate
boys and girls. She would discuss the crops or rag rugs
or the children and their need of a teacher with the adults,
ignoring the pigs and chickens underfoot. She seemed

to understand these sensitive and not easily approachable mountain people and soon won their confidence.

Lou Hoover discovered that contact with American education had been so spasmodic in the past that it had left few traces in the Kentucky mountains. Characteristically, she set about to try to remedy the situation. She told her husband, "A good school could help to awaken the mountain people from their two-century sleep and fit them into the pattern of the twentieth century."

She and Bert had decided to build the Dark Hollow schoolhouse and to hire a teacher at their own expense. She had planned for a small apartment to be attached to the school where the teacher could live. Now, six months later, there were thirty happy mountain children starting their formal education with Miss Christine Vest. "We were fortunate to find Miss Vest," Lou Hoover told a friend, "because she is a Kentucky mountain woman herself, trained at Berea College where the students earn their own tuition by farm work or making native products, such as jams. She is thoroughly devoted to her work and imbued with the spirit to serve. She has already had experience working with mountain folk and understands their limitations and idiosyncrasies."

The President came up to Rapidan each weekend while she was there. She knew that the camp was especially good for him while he was grappling with history-making problems that weighed heavily on his mind and heart. She planned for him to have as many weekends as possible there, with its assurance of rest, beauty, and brightness. And she remembered that many great newsworthy events were influenced by the lovely mountain camp; prophetic conferences between Herbert Hoover and Ramsay MacDonald had had a pleasing afterglow in their informal chats while seated on a log beside the trout stream. Key men of the Cabinet and various commissions had relaxed by building dams or bridges, after helping to shape coming events. Mrs. Hoover was especially reluctant to close the camp for the winter that year, but deep snow and impassable roads left her no alternative.

She carried to Washington a number of letters from farm women in the area, who complained bitterly about the persistent agricultural depression, and asked for her help. Some of the 4-H Club leaders also appealed to her. They told her how they had lost their farms and how rapidly falling farm prices made it impossible for them to pay their taxes. Lou Hoover personally answered every letter and told how the President had set up a Farm Board with the power and funds to aid the orderly marketing of crops. She carried the distress of the farm women in her heart as she turned to her own family problems.

Lou Hoover was anguished when her elder son became ill and wished she could arrange to be close beside him. Herbert had contracted tuberculosis. It was diagnosed in September and he spent the next couple of months at Camp Rapidan. In November, he was sent to a sanatorium in Asheville, North Carolina, to spend ten months in bed. His wife, Peggy, with the three children, Peggy Ann, Peter, and Joan, came to live at the White House to be near him.

A fireproof nursery for the children was set up on the third floor of the White House by their grandmother, who provided small tables, dressers, beds, and hooked rugs in the rooms allotted to Peggy Ann and Peter. Small Joan, with her own nurse, was installed in a room equipped with everything a baby needed.

On Christmas Eve, Mrs. Hoover and her grandchildren welcomed their mother, who flew up from Asheville to tuck the trio into bed at the White House after enjoying their tree and toys. Later, Peggy Hoover returned to the Blue Briar Cottage on a Carolina mountain slope to be with her husband on Christmas Day.

Even though Lou Hoover was involved in ceaseless official duties, as the winter passed she found time every day to enjoy her grandchildren. The week before Easter, 1931, she took Peggy Ann and Peter to Asheville to visit their parents, but made sure that they were back in Washington in time to welcome the hundreds of little guests to the executive grounds for the annual Easter egg roll the day after Easter.

Under dismal skies and showers, Lou and Bert Hoover valiantly defied the weather to attend Easter sunrise services at Arlington Cemetery. The program was cut short as the first family, along with 10,000 other people, fled the amphitheater in a big downpour.

An enormous crowd welcomed the President and First Lady in Springfield, Illinois, on June 17, where they went to rededicate Abraham Lincoln's remodeled tomb. Lou Hoover heard her husband picture Lincoln as a "symbol of union and human rights, whose stature in world history is steadily growing." After the speech she entered the tomb and placed a wreath there which had been presented by the Girl Scouts. Then she visited the old Lincoln home. It was furnished largely as it had been when Abraham Lincoln took leave of his neighbors to go to Washington.

Another stop on this trip was at Marion, Ohio, to dedicate the Memorial Tomb of Warren G. Harding.

In July, a much improved Herbert and Peggy took the children back to California. The President and First Lady had decided that they would remain in Washington all summer, foregoing any vacation trip because of the economic situation. She read with dismay that twenty-seven railroads were having financial trouble, that gold was being shipped from New York to Europe to reduce an oversupply, and that people were generally skimping or had stopped buying. Greatly disturbed by the loss of confidence throughout the country, she heard a radio commentator say, "Eight million people cannot buy, forty million will not buy, and prosperity will never return until the buying power of the country is restored."

Immediately she ordered new curtains for the White House and advised other women to buy what they could to help the merchants.

Part of the Administration's struggle to combat the depression was the creation of the Reconstruction Finance Corporation, which loaned money to banks, railroads, insurance companies, shipbuilders, and other industrial concerns to be used as working capital. Many new commercial ventures were started with the aid of this fund. The First Lady was interested in having a part in one of these ventures when, introduced as "the President's Chief of Staff," the First Lady christened the 7,000-ton cargo and passenger ship, the *Excalibur*, at Camden in July. At the luncheon that followed, a half-dozen speakers accepted the launching as a symbol and the christening by the First Lady of the Land as the happy forecast of the steady increase in American shipping upon the seven seas.

The United States was still hard hit by the depression, but Lou hoped the slump was over. She perceived the tremendous physical and psychological strains upon the President as he worked unremittingly trying to solve the long-growing problems which had caused the economic decline. She kept the weekends at Rapidan as peaceful and restful as possible for her husband by asking their guests to discuss neither government nor politics.

Official Washington curtailed its manner of entertaining, but carried on the prescribed program with smaller, less expensive parties.

The pinch of the depression was being felt widely and people were timid. Lou sensed this in Buffalo when she attended the National Girl Scout convention in August 1931. During the convention, she offered her opinion with regard to improving economic conditions.

"The women of the country are half the people in it," she said. "The ones who are not in trouble will have to help the ones who are. One way is to keep on living a normal life. We should not curtail too many activities that are essential, because otherwise we throw the whole machine out of gear. If we stop buying things we need, employment will drop tremendously."

Mrs. Hoover chose a psychological moment, a time when, by the consensus of opinion, things were on the upgrade, to urge a sensible spending of money by those who had it.

"There is no reason at all for just feeling sorry for ourselves over our present economic social problems. But there is every reason for each one of us to help solve the problems near us."

Editorial comments on Lou's statements were widely publicized. "These few sentences spoken by Mrs. Hoover might well be framed and hung up in our homes, shops, banks, and factories for they have the peculiar sanity that the world itself holds to," said the Chattanooga *Times*.

There was scarcely an empty hour on Lou's calendar, but one Sunday she left Rapidan early enough to accompany her husband to see a World Series baseball game because it was a favorite relaxation for him.

Following the game, she accompanied the President to Cleveland and listened to his address to the American Bankers Association, in which he reviewed the depression and declared the slump was over. The bankers received his words well, but Lou was struck by the unprecedented silence of the large throngs of people who crowded the four miles of Cleveland's Euclid Avenue as the official party proceeded to their hotel. She wondered if the un-enthusiastic attitude of the public was owing to the in-dustrial depression which had been particularly severe in Cleveland, or to political feuds, or to the general dis-satisfaction throughout the country on Prohibition and similar subjects. None knew as well as she how fiercely the President was grappling with these problems, and she was glad for the telegrams of congratulation that he re-ceived for his Cleveland speech, because sickening ap-prehension had been clutching at her heart as she came to the realization that public confidence in the Hoover administration was sagging. But she was not prepared for the official statement of the Federal Council of Churches of Christ in America, which was read from the pulpits on Labor Day Sunday. It was a sweeping indictment of American capitalism.

In October, when Lou Hoover read in the newspapers about the financial crash in Europe, she was making plans for the coming of distinguished visitors from there. M. Pierre Laval, Premier of France, and his daughter were to be guests at the White House. Premier Laval, in a con-ventional black cutaway coat and wearing a high silk hat, was met at the dock by Ambassador M. Claudel and General John J. Pershing, commander of American forces during the war. After formalities of a state dinner and reception were over, the two heads of state had heart-to-heart talks in the Lincoln study.

Pretty nineteen-year-old Mlle. Josée Laval arrived at the White House in a becoming costume of blue corduroy with a hat of the same hue. Later she shed a few tears and finally told her hostess that she was heartbroken and wished to take the first boat back to France. Soon Mrs. Hoover discovered the reason for her grief. It was because the protocol demanded by some top-hat official did not allow her to see the Navy-Princeton football game in Palmer Stadium, which she had looked forward to doing. However, she dried her tears when understanding Lou Hoover promised a date for her with one of the players. After a dinner party with some young people, the group went to get a look at the city from the top of Washington Monument which was opened especially for Lou and her guests.

Eventually, Mrs. Hoover learned that her husband and the French Premier confined their talks largely to discussion of policies that could cut short the depression. They also laid the groundwork for revision of the war debt and agreed on steps to bring about a better world economic stability. M. Laval told the First Lady how grateful he was for Mr. Hoover's distribution of food and clothing to thousands of destitute French people during the war. She was pleased when the Premier declared his mission in Washington was a success.

The holiday season was approaching, but Lou Hoover contrived to sandwich the required number of fifteen-minute sittings into her crowded schedule to permit the famous artist, Philip A. de Laszlo, to paint her portrait.

She was happy because both of her sons were coming to Washington to spend the holidays. A few days before Christmas, spirited Peggy Ann and Peter took over the White House and with their grandmother's help planned for the annual children's party. Baby Joan remained in Palo Alto with her maternal grandmother, being too young for the long journey.

"We want a lot of people to come," said Peggy Ann,

"because this year they will bring presents to the party instead of getting them. Grandmother is going to give all the toys and clothes to boys and girls in Washington who need them."

Lou Hoover ordered special dishes for the young guests, to be prepared in the White House kitchen, before she took her grandchildren shopping for the party. They went to several shops, including a five-and-ten-cent store, and bought games, dolls, and toys. Both customers and clerks in some of the stores failed to recognize the informal shoppers.

Following Christmas, the first family gave a dance at the White House for Allan, who was honor guest. A new wrist fad was started that night, when the First Lady wore a small bouquet of red rosebuds attached to a chiffon ribbon around her wrist. Each of the girl guests was presented with similar bouquets and ribbons. The girls liked the idea so well that the florists in Washington were soon swamped with demands for wrist bouquets instead of corsages.

"What is Allan doing now?" one of the guests asked Mrs. Hoover.

"He has gone to work in a lower clerical position in a branch bank in Los Angeles," she was told.

"Why?" persisted the guest, "when his father could have appointed him to a big job in the government?"

"Allan is too independent to accept favors that he has not earned," replied his mother, not without pride, "and he prefers to make his own way in life."

XIV

EFFECTS OF THE GREAT DEPRESSION

•

1932

THE WIDESPREAD CONSEQUENCES of the depression weighed heavily on Lou Hoover and she planned to keep all entertaining as simple as possible. What should I wear for the New Year reception? she wondered.

For this daytime affair at the White House she chose a most becoming gown of tête-de-tête negre velvet and tulle in alternate pointed bands. With it she wore a short jacket of velvet, disclosing a bit of beige lace on the bodice. She wore no hat.

Those two engaging grandchildren, Peggy Ann and Peter, nearly stole the show as the annual New Year reception got under way on January 1, 1932. Both dressed in blue linen with smocking, they appeared under the escort of Mrs. Dare Stark McMullin, White House guest from Palo Alto. They took their places in the Green Room doorway, jumping up and down in their excitement as the President and First Lady made their way downstairs. Mrs. Hoover turned and waved a greeting to the pair, who wigwagged madly back to her, their small faces alight.

Fewer than usual people came to the reception and

there was much talk of how to relieve the poverty-stricken people in America.

In the middle of January, Ignace Jan Paderewski arrived to tour the country and he told Lou Hoover that he would like to give some concerts for the benefit of the unemployed in the United States.

"There is a certain appropriateness," he told her, "in the fact that I, the former Polish Premier, offer my services to the wife of the man who directed famine relief in Poland."

Mrs. Hoover arranged for Paderewski to give a Washington concert on January 25, and for four other concerts in New York, Boston, Philadelphia, and Chicago, the proceeds to be administered by the Red Cross.

"Mr. Paderewski's five concerts," she explained, "will be the eminent pianist's eloquent gesture of good will toward a country which came to the aid of his own stricken people during the war."

Paderewski was a guest in the White House, where a special piano was installed in an upper suite for him. Here he played for hours while Lou Hoover, members of the White House staff, and the gardeners paused in their work to listen, fascinated by the glorious flood of music pouring from the upper windows.

Ovations and encores marked the Washington concert, and Lou Hoover, as sponsor of the event, sent a check for $11,852 to the American Red Cross with a note saying that "Mr. Paderewski very especially wishes it to purchase food for Americans hungry and in distress, so if you can see that it quite certainly goes for that purpose we will be carrying out the wishes of the generous donor."

People of all ages were asked to help in fighting the depression. In a radio talk to thousands of young 4-H

Club members, Mrs. Hoover called upon the boys and girls of the nation to do their part with confidence and courage. She urged them to be helpful to their neighbors in unfortunate circumstances and to learn how to do without things cheerfully, instead of submitting to an aimless day-to-day fretful worry. She suggested that they make more use of the materials at hand in the United States, and as an example directed their attention to the active campaign of research and promotion which was endeavoring to discover new uses for American cotton.

She immediately put her preaching into practice when she appeared at a formal White House reception in the evening attired in a cotton gown. The occasion was the last official appearance of Andrew W. Mellon, soon to be ambassador to the Court of St. James's. The center of attention at the party shifted from Mr. Mellon, who had served as Secretary of the Treasury for eleven years and under three Presidents, to Lou Hoover and her cotton dress.

The pictorial character of the dress aroused interest from the moment she appeared. It was fashioned of blue-and-white sprigged muslin after an old painting and closely resembled a gown worn by her mother in the late seventies. The bodice was tight-fitting, with short ruffled sleeves, and the skirt with its train was ruffled to the waistline. In keeping with the period of her costume, Lou Hoover wore a black velvet bow in her silvery hair, which was dressed lower than usual. About her throat was a black velvet band. Her lorgnette hung from a narrow black ribbon and a small black velvet handbag completed her most unusual and becoming costume.

The First Lady's cotton evening gown was described in the newspapers and pictured in the newsreels, and her patriotism was generally praised.

"Mrs. Herbert Hoover started something," said an editorial in the San Francisco *Chronicle*. "Not only has Mrs. Hoover's original idea startled the fashion experts, but it has also won hearty cheers from the cotton textile industry, which is making an intensive campaign to popularize cotton and American-made rayon in place of silk. The campaign is now receiving impetus by American women everywhere as an economic slap at the depression."

Reports that Mrs. Hoover had appeared in a cotton gown instead of silk for a state function tempted the *Manchester Guardian,* usually a staid British journal, to speculate facetiously on the possibilities of "grave international complications" with Japan.

The White House hostess continued her social duties, faithfully and wholeheartedly. In addition to the dinners and receptions of tradition, she daily received groups of women involved in official life and in organizations and answered many a call of charity. Visitors thronged the Capitol for the opening of the bicentennial celebration of Washington's birthday. The President and First Lady attended services at Old Christ Church in Alexandria, where Washington had worshiped and from which he was buried.

Later that day, Mrs. Hoover granted an interview to a small group of visiting magazine writers who wanted her views on the economic depression and what women could do to counteract it. She told them that the crisis in the social system was something for which no individual could be held responsible. She said that in the aftermath of the war there was disintegration and collapse of whole financial systems in several European countries, one after another, and it could not fail to react upon the United States. She urged that women cease to hoard, that they wear cotton clothes, and that the women in each community do everything possible to aid the local people who needed help. She also suggested cooperative ventures, repair of clothing, and trade by barter or exchange within a community.

Among the many activities that claimed her attention, the First Lady was honorary president of the women's committee of the National Cathedral Association. She entertained at a special White House tea for the two hundred visitors from all over the country who had done their bit toward the building of the great house of worship in Washington. She rearranged her Sunday so that she could represent the first family at the morning service, marking the formal opening of the great sanctuary of the Washington Cathedral.

"This is one place where I can appear for Bert," she told the bishop. "You know his physician, Dr. Joel T. Boone, has forbidden him to participate, for several months at least, in periods of extended handshaking."

The formal White House statement said, "Mrs. Hoover will be delighted whenever possible to extend the courtesies of the White House to visiting organizations, the official members of which wish to be received."

These were days of great strain on the President, and his wife was worried when she saw his face drawn with weariness or observed his tired walk. I must plan a vacation for him, she thought and began to map out a rest trip to Florida. But in the end she went without him.

Early in March, the First Lady and her party were cruising in South Atlantic coastal waters on the motorship *Sequoia*, a Department of Commerce inland waterways inspection boat, and had anchored in the St. Johns River. Newspapers brought from the shore carried President Hoover's unequivocal pronouncement in favor of

Prohibition repeal and told of the electric effect this had on the entire country. Leaders of finance and labor, commerce and industry, were quoted, hailing this as marking the inevitable turning point in the nation's economic struggle. Exuberant celebrations in the streets were described, and in a long-distance telephone conversation Bert Hoover told his wife, "The Democrats think I have stolen their thunder."

The First Lady's Southern itinerary included a visit to St. Augustine, Savannah, Miami, and Jacksonville before returning to Washington. As always, she was delighted by the tributes of lovely flowers offered her. The cruise was marred by the tragic news about the kidnaping of the Lindbergh baby. Lou Hoover kept in close touch with Anne Lindbergh and at every dock telephoned for latest news of the nationwide hunt for the kidnaper. With a catch in her voice, she offered her personal services to the mother of blond, curly-haired Charles, Jr., son of the Lone Eagle. The baby was pitilessly being held for ransom, while a great wave of indignation swept through the whole nation.

With her genuine friendliness, the First Lady made a deep impression on the South. In this time of political tension she was happy to read in the *Washington Star:*

> The First Lady of the land has furnished the best possible example of the indirect method of fostering the success of the Republicans in the South. Not a Southerner, Mrs. Hoover is exactly the type of womanhood to enlist the interests of Southern women. She is direct, soft-spoken, altogether unpretentious, and carries out the old Southern tradition of confidence in one's own standing. Wherever she went she was received with the warmhearted hospitality that glows best south of the Mason-Dixon Line.

Mrs. Hoover came home to a big stack of mail. Every week from all over the country she received letters from parents asking for help to keep their children in school. The main difficulty, according to the letters, was that the children lacked proper clothes and there was no money with which to buy necessary books. Lou Hoover asked the cooperation of the National Congress of Parents and Teachers and answered every letter received. Often she advised the writer to apply to the local parent-teacher association for help.

She continued to be recognized in academic circles, as her seventh honorary degree was awarded on May 14, at Wooster, Ohio. The degree of Doctor of Letters and Humanities was given in recognition of her work in social service. She was especially delighted because her great-grandfather, William Henry, was one of the three men who laid out the settlement and the college ceremony coincided with the 125th anniversary celebration of the founding of the town. The First Lady was becoming accustomed to standing beneath stately campus elms and oaks with a mortarboard on her head, but she was quite impressed by the more than five thousand spectators who attended the Wooster College event. At the luncheon in her honor, President Charles F. Wishart said, "I want to congratulate you upon the choice of your great-grandfather, who, when he came West, knew where and when to stop."

In a letter to her uncle, William Henry, she described the day; a genuine glimpse of Americana.

May 24, 1932

My dear Uncle Will,

It was all a tremendously interesting celebration. I do wish you might have been there, and I know the people of

Wooster regretted your absence very much. When we arrived on the morning of the 14th, it was drizzling, and it seemed such a shame that all the plans should be endangered.

I had taken along three palm sprays, which were placed early, during a little drive, at the Monument to the three Founders, which stands at one side of the Market Square. We drove through the nice old streets and finally came to the cemetery, where I put wreaths of magnolia and palm leaves—a largish one on our tall central Henry monument, and four smaller ones on the four headstones. Then back to the house of President Wishart of the college.

It was still damp and overcast, but by delaying the college program for about an hour, we were rewarded by bright sunlight for the rest of the day. The Color Day ceremony and Goethe Pageant at the College Stadium were too lovely—the gay costumes and very well-enacted scenes standing out against the green of the far slopes. After the Pageant, I was presented with a degree, and many much too nice things were said about me! Then we hurried on to a luncheon where I met all the faculty and trustees of the college, as well as many friends who had come to Wooster just for the day.

After luncheon was the Historical Pageant at the Fair Grounds. It was splendidly done, and you would have loved all the old costumes and the oxcart and real old carts and wagons and covered wagons and real stagecoaches, and buggies and buckboards, that had been unearthed for the performance. And many horses! I was told that most of the dresses and suits worn by the players were actually ones that had been found in attics and old trunks. They were priceless and very lovely.

I had to leave the Pageant before it was quite finished, as there was a tea scheduled for me, where I met about three hundred of the members of committees and various of the real old townspeople, many of whom had known you and Mother and Father.

Then a dash for the train to Washington, and one of the most pleasant and interesting days I have ever spent was over.[1]

As a pleasant prelude to evening ceremonies, on June 22 Lou Hoover gave a small, intimate dinner at the White House for Amelia Earhart, the first woman to make a solo flight across the Atlantic, and her husband, George Palmer Putnam. Also present was Gilbert Grosvenor, president of the National Geographic Society, which was to bestow a special gold medal on Amelia. President Hoover made the presentation following the dinner. A notable audience of diplomats and statesmen, officers of the Army and Navy, and civilians, witnessed the colorful event at Constitution Hall.

Lou Hoover particularly admired this young woman who had the courage to accomplish seemingly impossible ventures, and for the first time in many weeks went to bed in happy forgetfulness of the depression.

During these days the First Lady read with dismay the newspaper accounts of hunger marches and a serious riot of unemployed persons in Dearborn, Michigan. And how the farmers in Iowa and the Middle West had organized to prevent mortgage owners from profiting by foreclosure. Then she began to see ragged members of the so-called Bonus Expeditionary Force on the streets of Washington and heard that they were building a shanty town on Anacostia Flats outside the city. These thousands of unemployed war veterans had gathered to demand immediate payments of bonus money scheduled for several months later. White House gatherings were full of discussions of this situation as the President held conferences with

[1] This letter is in the Lou Henry Hoover archives at the Hoover Institution, Stanford.

leaders of the great public-works programs and industries to try to increase employment. Lou Hoover heard her husband plead that industry strain every effort to create new employment by undertaking new construction and improvements, and to put human well-being first and profits last.

She was relieved when Congress appropriated funds for transportation, and about half of the Bonus Expeditionary Force left Washington and went home. But she was increasingly distressed by the organized smear campaign against her husband and his leadership which was carried on during the spring and summer. In spite of this, the Republican convention nominated him for re-election.

In preparation for the busy week of notification ceremonies, Mrs. Hoover persuaded the President to spend a few days at Camp Rapidan. A little later, on August 10, the Chief Executive celebrated his fifty-eighth birthday by going to work as usual. But his wife saw to it that the day did not pass unnoticed. She arranged for a huge birthday cake with plenty of colorful icing and candles to grace the dinner table that evening. The cake was made in the White House kitchen under the personal supervision of the First Lady and was ornamented with the words "Happy Birthday" on top.

The next day, Mrs. Hoover completed preparations for a garden party and luncheon at the White House for four hundred guests who had come to Washington for the notification of the President's nomination. Later, Constitution Hall was crowded with some four thousand guests, invited from official and diplomatic society, political organizations, and ardent Republican supporters. Lou Hoover listened closely to the notification ceremonies, marked by speeches full of loyalty and respect for the Chief Executive.

She heard recognition of the President's heroic struggle to protect the weak and succor the stricken during his long fight to defeat the depression. And she heard praise for his resolve to preserve the consciousness of individual responsibility for every man and woman to help the less fortunate, and for his refusal to allow political domination of the Red Cross. None better than she knew that he deserved the thanks he received for forcing rigid economy upon all federal departments, to reduce a huge tax burden, and the credit for bringing about better mutual understanding between the United States and other countries by fighting isolationism.

In the days following the ceremonies, Lou Hoover was acutely aware of the intensified "Smear Hoover" campaign and of the many untrue statements being published about her husband, but while seething inwardly she continued to go about her daily round of duties with her usual outward calm.

Consistent with her deep interest in welfare activities, Lou went to the aid of community chests. In September, she was named honorary chairman of a National Woman's Committee with one thousand members organized to back the current year's welfare and relief campaign launched from the White House. She invited a group of committee members to the White House to talk over plans.

"Food and warmth and health are not enough to satisfy the desires of life," stated Lou Hoover. "Occupation and recreation are as vital to those harassed by trouble as to the carefree. Therefore, we should redouble our efforts to supply educational and recreational opportunities and the activities given by what we call character-building organizations."

Lou Hoover spent a colorful October of personal contact with the voters and always close to her husband's side. Vivid were the memory pictures she carried of the many campaign trips. Cleveland was a moonlit city, with a great illuminated tower in the center and four crowd-filled auditoriums to be successively visited. Noisy Detroit, echoing first with "boos" from crowds near the station, bearing banners marked, "Workers Ex-Service Men's League," later gave a prolonged ovation at the auditorium.

Across Illinois, Indiana, Ohio, and Pennsylvania the First Lady campaigned with her husband, doing something personal to make the crowds happy at each stop. At Chicago and Fort Wayne she greeted the people and then stepped aside to permit the children to see the President more clearly. At Lima, Ohio, when the megaphone man couldn't make himself heard from the clamor, she held up two fingers, said "Sh-h-h," and got the people quieted down.

On another Midwest trip, in the midst of smiling and waving to the crowds at Des Moines, Iowa, she warned them, "A lot of little boys and girls are down here in front. Don't you big people push in and get them crushed." These spontaneous gestures were most effective because it was obvious that they were warmly sincere.

With enough flowers to decorate the whole White House, personal gifts from people in a score of towns, and a bushel basket of Maryland apples for good measure, Lou Hoover returned to Washington with her husband for a brief stay before starting off to a Madison Square Garden rally in New York.

During the six weeks of campaigning, the First Lady traveled 12,000 miles and slept twenty nights in railroad trains. She made no campaign speeches but many times she talked from the rear platform to the station crowds as they invariably called for her after the President had spoken. She always responded with some happy reference to the people themselves and their community, and directed her talks especially to the mothers and children.

En route to Palo Alto, where she expected to vote on November 8, Lou Hoover, in accord with her usual hospitality, decided it would be enjoyable to hold open house on San Juan Hill to add to the interest of receiving election returns. She telegraphed to Allan, who was at his parents' home, to arrange for a bountiful supper and call in the neighbors and friends.

It was heartwarming for Lou and Bert Hoover to arrive in Palo Alto and see the tremendous "Welcome Home" banners in the streets and on their campus home. In the windows of hundreds of stores and private houses were large pictures of the President draped with the national colors. Along the way, she loved seeing once more the bright-berried toyon bushes and the profusion of fall flowers.

A throng that had stood waiting for more than an hour cheered enthusiastically as the car swung into University Avenue and drew up to the improvised stand upon which were gathered the City Council of Palo Alto. Mayor Earl Thomas greeted the First Lady and the President, and Girl Scouts presented a bouquet of flowers. Scores of people lined Palm Drive, and the Stanford University Band led the way to the second part of the reception in front of Memorial Court on the campus. Hundreds of students and townspeople crowded the stairs and lawns, filled the windows, and covered the roofs of the buildings looking down on the court. In the absence of Ray Lyman Wilbur, the acting president of Stanford, Dr. Robert E. Swain, and Dean Theodore J. Hoover, the President's brother and executive head of the School of Engineering, greeted the first family on behalf of the University. Lou looked appreciatively at her old college campus with its countless pepper trees heavy with red pods, and the many drooping palm trees. Soon her heart skipped as she caught a glimpse of her own well-loved home and saw that powerful floodlights were focused upon it from all four corners. Later, she found installed inside, in her sewing room, a switchboard equipped to serve forty telephone lines. She was told that sixteen lines had been installed for the press and radio reporters next door.

She immediately opened several boxes containing much-battered toys to be ready for the expected visit of Peggy Ann, Peter, and Joan. Among the other members of the family who had gathered at San Juan Hill were Lou's sister and uncle, Jean Henry Large and William D. Henry, and Jean's son and daughter, Delano and Janet Large. Theodore Hoover and his sister, May Hoover Leavitt, joined them later in the day to complete the family guest list. While playing her usual part of perfect hostess to relatives and friends, the First Lady remained close to the Chief Executive as the returns from the polls came into their home. Intimate friends who joined the family in watching the blackboard in the reception room whispered to each other and shook their heads glumly as state after state gave greater leads to Franklin Delano Roosevelt. With a sinking heart, solemn-faced Lou Hoover sadly watched her husband's political house go crashing down about him, but she held out hope to the last.

The lawn outside was bright as day under the floodlights. About midnight, when Secret Service men, newspaper reporters, and photographers began gathering into little groups preparing to leave, Mrs. Hoover heard the President say, "We believe the American people have the right to make their own decision. We will all abide by it like good Americans." Then she turned to her secretary and put her head down on Mildred Hall's shoulder without saying a word.

The next day, the wife of the President and his gallant companion in many strenuous campaign trips shared with him the quiet of their beloved campus home and smilingly directed household activities. She spent part of the morning on the roof sun porch, overlooking the east lawn, watching Peggy Ann and Peter splash around in the swimming pool below, under the watchful eyes of their mother. She read the newspapers and, in between, called their grandfather's attention to the antics of the children.

Outwardly Lou Hoover's spirits were undampened by the defeat of her husband in the presidential election. Part of the day she devoted to answering letters and telegrams, and she gave a skillful touch to the arranging of many of the profuse floral gifts still coming in from personal friends. It was her first opportunity in nearly four years to be out-of-doors in her own rose garden and an unusually warm November day made it especially enjoyable.

To her sons, Mrs. Hoover expressed concern about their father's need for rest after the long strain of campaigning on top of his arduous and exacting duties as the President of the United States. She told them with pride that his present mood was philosophical in the face of defeat and that this quality had always enabled him to stand up under hard pressure and recover quickly from fatigue or disappointment. "He will work tremendously to accomplish an object," she said, "but having put everything he has into the fight, if it finally goes against him, he accepts the result and does not try to dictate forever to eternal Providence."

The driveway leading to the house was chained off and a California state policeman had orders to bar those not having particular business, including newspapermen. The mistress of the San Juan Hill home appreciated the almost complete quiet of this day in contrast to the bustle, clamor, and crowds of the previous day. Herbert, Jr., who was teaching business economics and aeronautics at the California Institute of Technology in Pasadena, urged his mother to visit him and Peggy in their new home at Sierra Madre before leaving the state. When her sons left, she began to think ahead to all that she wanted to accomplish in Washington during the coming three months.

For the next few days Lou Hoover busied herself in re-establishing old friendships on the university campus and in preparing their home for the return of Bert and herself after the inauguration of the next President. She renewed her membership in the Red Cross at the start of its local annual drive and received her button from Mrs. Bailey Willis, wife of the Professor Emeritus of Geology at Stanford and close friend of the family.

Refreshed after their vacation days in the old home, the President and First Lady returned to Washington where they were greeted in defeat by cheering thousands of "home folk" who ignored the police lines at Union Station in their effort to express a hearty welcome. An enthusiastic crowd, estimated by the police at from three thousand to five thousand persons, crashed the train shed gates and lined themselves up along the full length of the presidential train. Obviously moved, the recipients of this popular reception were forced to make their way through a friendly mob intent on shaking hands. A woman pushed her way through the throng and presented Lou with a huge bouquet of yellow roses from the League of Republican Women.

A quiet Thanksgiving was observed by the White House family in 1932 just as it was by millions of other Ameri-

cans, with church attendance, followed by a turkey dinner.
The First Lady and the President attended the Thanksgiving Day services at the Foundry Methodist Episcopal
Church on Sixteenth Street and a few close friends from
official life were invited in for dinner in the evening.
These included cabinet officers and their wives, Ray
Lyman Wilbur, William N. Doak, Roy Chapin, and
Charles F. Adams. Most of these guests were observing
the last Thanksgiving in their official positions. They
talked about what they would miss when they left Washington and what they could do to help pull the country
out of the depression when they arrived at their own
homes.

On the way home from church that morning, Mrs.
Hoover had seen a crowd of people milling around in the
street by the East Gate to the White House. "Look, Bert,
the police are arresting some men," she exclaimed. "Who
do you suppose they are?"

As the official car came closer to the disturbance, Bert
replied, "Those are some leaders of the Hunger March."

His wife's throat tightened and she felt ill. Now I know
what I shall talk about tomorrow, she thought.

In her radio broadcast from the White House the next
day, Lou Hoover urged all women to increase their relief
efforts in the war against poverty and serve as volunteers
in the work of the National Welfare Committee to end
the suffering of needy people during the winter.

"My plea is," she urged, "that our most important duty
is to find when, how, and where people need help. The
winter is upon us. We cannot be warm, in the house or
out, we cannot sit down to a table sufficiently supplied
with food, if we do not know that it is possible for every
child, woman, and man in the United States also to be
sufficiently warmed and fed." There was a little break

in her voice as she concluded: "We must give not only a helping hand, but a willing ear and an understanding heart to those about us in little or great need through no fault of their own."

On a cold December morning, Lou turned up the fur collar of her coat and stepped into her car to go to the workrooms of the Red Cross. So few official days are left, she thought, and I want to do what little I can to help with the tremendous amount that needs to be done. She was headed for a room where fellow volunteers had mastered the control of thirty whirring sewing machines, mostly antiquated models that had been donated for the cause. They were converting Federal Farm Board cotton into clothes for the poor children in the national capital, dresses for the girls and shirts for the boys.

At the same time, she did not forget her California home town. On December 11, the Palo Alto unemployment relief fund acknowledged a contribution from Mrs. Herbert Hoover, "to be used to employ local residents who are urgently in need of jobs."

One day toward the middle of December, when Lou Hoover returned to the White House from the Red Cross workroom, she observed with a pang how worn and weary her husband looked. She knew how harassed he was by the scourge of reproaches from his political enemies, who sought by implication to place on him the entire blame for the depression. Lou Hoover knew well that this blame could not be placed fairly on her husband. She knew that the decline had started long before he became President, and further economic deterioration could be attributed to the delays in Congress, failure to cooperate with sound proposals to bolster the national credit, and to financial storms in Europe.

She went quickly to him and took his arm. "You need

to get away from your desk and your work, dear," she told him. "Why can't we take ten days for a Christmas holiday and go to Florida for a deep-sea fishing cruise?"

"All right," he agreed halfheartedly, "go ahead and arrange it."

A few minutes after leaving their train at Long Key, the Hoover party boarded the yacht *Saunterer*, chartered for the vacation, and sailed off into the blue Gulf of Mexico.

Day after day they sailed out into deep waters where the fishing was good. Lou Hoover watched her husband closely as he battled with big barracudas, bonitas, and sailfish in the blazing semi-tropic sun and landed his treasures with boyish enthusiasm. And she noted with satisfaction that his face, now ruddy with sunburn, wore a more and more relaxed expression.

XV

PRIVATE CITIZEN

•

1933–1939

BACK IN THE CAPITAL after the restful holiday in Florida,
the First Lady's plans for official entertaining were interrupted by the shocking suddenness of the death of former
President Calvin Coolidge on January 8, 1933. By proclamation of President Hoover, Washington observed a
thirty-day period of mourning and the Hoovers had to
cancel dinners for the Vice President, the Diplomatic
Corps, and the Chief Justice, after invitations had already
been mailed. The rest of the curtailed schedule was easier
to manage. Following the mourning period, there were
only three weeks left before the inauguration of a new
administration and the introduction of a new hostess in
the White House.

Lou Hoover planned carefully for the few remaining
social events that would take place before she and her
husband left the Executive Mansion, but her thoughts
naturally turned more and more often to the time of her
return to Palo Alto. It was with mixed emotions that she
looked forward to the fast-approaching day, March 4,
when Bert would again become a private citizen. She

longed for the opportunity to live serenely in their lovely hilltop home on the Stanford campus and to have Bert free from the terrible strains of the past four years. But she knew that, for him, there could be no more poignant moment than that in which he surrendered the power and responsibility of the Presidency of the United States.

The new life would call for many readjustments of outlook and interests, but she hoped that relief from the tremendous responsibility of planning for a whole nation would work its cure for him. Her own saddest parting was with Camp Rapidan. Here she had been her genuine self and had enjoyed the companionship of friends, both old and new. She talked it over with Bert one morning as they lingered over their breakfast coffee.

"There will never be another place like Camp Rapidan," she began. "I'll always remember the big fireplace, the walks through the woods, and the lovely stream. What a wonderful place it was to entertain informally! I think it was valuable when I remember how many of our official guests responded to relaxation that liberated them from rigid formalities in old-fashioned shirt-sleeve comfort. Do you realize that we put up fifteen buildings on those 165 acres as we developed that camp site?"

"Yes," he replied, "and you did a fine job of planning the whole thing." Then, watching her closely, he asked, "How would you like to deed the entire property to the federal government to be incorporated in Shenandoah National Park and made available for future Presidents and their cabinets, as our gift?" [1]

This was agreed upon. They also made the firm decision that he would not seek public office again and that they would go back to California to live permanently.

[1] Camp Rapidan was partially restored for use in 1962. The Roosevelts made no use of the camp and the buildings deteriorated.

About the middle of February, Lou Hoover invited Eleanor Roosevelt to come to the White House, to see what furniture the new first family would need to bring with them, since most of the household articles in the President's living quarters belonged to the Hoovers.

Lou Hoover's days were very full as she supervised the packing of the personal effects of the Hoover family, ranging from handbags to automoblies. At last she saw sixty-nine packages safely aboard the naval transport, *Henderson*, headed for San Francisco. Besides their own furniture and other personal effects, the shipment included many individual gifts made to the first family.

Although her daily mail was voluminous, Lou Hoover struggled to answer all the letters of multitudes of personal friends and well-wishers who expressed their affection and admiration for the first family.

On March 4, Lou Hoover went to the Inauguration and watched her husband accompany Franklin D. Roosevelt to the speaker's platform. "What will be the next thing for Bert?" she wondered.

She knew that he would never lead a life of idleness, but would become active again in business and in the affairs of his country. She admired the way he talked to his official family or to visitors, in a low tone and with not the slightest hint of rancor or bitterness, and her heart went out to him as she detected a certain wistfulness about him, particularly when he smiled. He seemed calm and philosophical, but she knew he was suppressing his real emotions.

Following the inaugural ceremony, Mr. and Mrs. Hoover went directly from the Capitol to the train. They traveled together as far as Philadelphia, then he went on to New York for a couple of weeks. She timed her journey to California so that she could travel with Herbert on his return journey from a business trip, and she planned to visit with his family at their new home in Sierra Madre until her husband could join her at Palo Alto.

Mildred Hall was on board the same train, with a maid for the campus home. She was in charge of the dogs, a canary, and all the baggage.

En route to California, Mrs. Hoover received the homage of several Kansas City organizations when she changed trains at Union Station.

"There will be time here to walk the dogs," she said, and started for the baggage car to get them. She and Miss Hall emerged with two—Pat, a police dog, and Weegie, a Norwegian elkhound—tugging at their leashes. They wanted to walk the dogs in the train sheds, but were immediately surrounded by clamoring crowds, so Mrs. Hoover turned Weegie over to Herbert. She caught sight of Scout uniforms and held out her hands to the girls who pushed through and gave her a box of flowers. They remembered, just in time, to salute.

She was told that people were waiting upstairs to see her. In the waiting room of the Union Station a great crowd had gathered and she was jostled by people eager to shake her hand. Loaded down with more flowers, she felt a jar of jelly pressed into her free hand. Everyone was talking to her at once. She was gracious to everyone who tried to speak to her, especially to the children, but she finally escaped and returned to the train sheds, so she could spend the last few minutes visiting with old friends.

On board the train once more, Lou Hoover read an editorial by Wills J. Abbot in the *Christian Science Monitor* that helped her understand the political situation.

If the Democrats in Congress should leave largely unchanged Mr. Hoover's plans for the reconstruction of the business structure, there might be a demand for recognition of his services. It is hardly likely, however, that Democratic policy will permit this. The party which out of office devoted so much attention to the successful endeavor to "smear Hoover" is not likely when in power to leave undone anything for the completion of that particular task.

Tears welled up in her eyes as she read the editorial of March 7 in the *New York Herald Tribune:*

To step down from high office as simply and with as complete courtesy and dignity as did Mr. Hoover, is in a great American tradition. But it nonetheless stirs a wave of admiration that deserves noting even in these crowded days. Let it be added that the reserved friendliness and the complete good taste with which Mrs. Hoover graced the White House were not less marked in her leaving. Wherever their future may lead them, here are two citizens of whom America can always feel proud.

Editorial note was also made of the fact that Mr. Hoover failed to draw his salary of $75,000 a year while he was President, and turned it all back into the Treasury and that he built the Rapidan camp at his own expense and gave it to the government.

When, finally, the Hoovers reached Palo Alto from that "perilous pitiless pinnacle" that was the White House, Lou Hoover appreciated the tranquility of their San Juan Hill home on the campus. At last she had plenty of time for friends, books, family, and fishing trips with her husband. Friends from the campus and the town kept her involved in many university and community activities. The Hoovers entertained not only their personal friends but also many campus organizations in their home. For example, the annual chrysanthemum student benefit tea given by the Stanford Mothers' Club originated at the Hoover residence and was held there each year from 1933 to 1938, when it outgrew even that spacious place.

Mrs. Hoover's genuine concern in all phases of university life led her to sponsor many other affairs which benefited the students' needs. She showed her personal interest by sending boxes of heart-shaped cookies to Stanford girls who announced their engagements, and in many other ways kept close to the school life in both the undergraduate and faculty circles.

Every day there was a mountain of mail intended to involve her in still more public activities, while some of it reflected the economic situation of the country with many appeals for advice or help. Certain letters were from professional chiselers, but many were from people who in their troubles turned to a lady they knew to be kindly and very resourceful, to answer pleas for personal advice and money. Others contained requests for pieces of Mr. Hoover's neckties, autographed photographs, and endorsements of products for advertising purposes. Lou Hoover usually devoted the time between her eight-o'clock breakfast on the terrace and noon to going through her personal letters herself. She kept in touch constantly with the swift-moving current of events.

Books demanded major time and pleasant attention. She enjoyed going through the new arrivals appraising the current reviews of these publications and she listed all those she thought her husband would like to read. For the most part, she omitted light fiction, but everything that could have any interest for the Hoover War Library she saved for him. Many documents dealing with the causes of World War I were accumulating in the Stanford library.

"The War Library is bulging," he told her. "There are boxes of manuscripts that cannot be shelved because the space is all used up. We need a special building for it."

The summer of 1934 brought the Hoovers a welcome visit from their grandchildren. Peggy Ann and Peter could hardly wait for their car to stop in the driveway to start racing for their grandmother. Lou Hoover gathered the squealing pair into her arms and then waited to include little Joan. There followed days filled with delightful activities of picnics and drives along the beautiful roads near Stanford, bordered with live oaks and sycamores. She watched the children romp through her own colorful terraced gardens with Weegie and Gretta, a new Norwegian elkhound, and held serious council with the youngsters about the naming of a new puppy.

When school time arrived and the grandchildren had returned home, Bert said, "Let's go trout fishing."

"Fine," responded Lou. "Where shall we go?"

"Some of my favorite haunts are along the Oregon rivers, so let's head north."

Lou Hoover joined in the preparations for the fishing trip with keen zest. She packed hiking shoes and fishing tackle. The congenial couple drove leisurely through northern California enjoying the giant redwood trees in Humboldt County and doing a little fishing in the Russian River. They camped out and cooked the fish they caught. Along the unspoiled Oregon beaches they found treasures of driftwood and beach agates.

At Gold Beach, Bert Hoover was elated. "Here is the mouth of the Rogue. There will be good fishing for thirty or forty miles up this river because here the trout maintain themselves naturally and grow large." He proved his point by catching a thirteen-pound Rainbow a couple of hours later.

After ten days, they returned to their home, bronzed and rested from their little informal vacation.

Lou Hoover liked the freedom of being a private citizen. She did her shopping in Palo Alto and was apt to pay by check without revealing her identity in advance. Sometimes unfamiliar saleswomen were startled by the name on the checks handed them by this quiet, unassuming customer.

Mrs. Hoover's lack of ostentation showed again when she was asked to contribute a dress to the Smithsonian Institution for its collection of historic gowns worn by the First Ladies of the Land. Instead of sending her elaborate inaugural gown, she sent a lovely dress of aquamarine satin. It was simply fashioned with a softly draped bodice and a skirt with pointed flounces. "This gown has no particular historical associations," she wrote in the accompanying letter. "It was just a dress that I enjoyed wearing, and for that reason I selected it from the others I wore while in the White House."

The Smithsonian request was followed later by one from Mrs. Roosevelt asking for a portrait to hang in the White House. For this purpose, Mrs. Hoover chose one painted by Miss Lydia Field Emmet of New York, at the invitation of the Girl Scouts, who wanted to present it to the White House in recognition of Mrs. Hoover's interest in that organization.

It was difficult for the former First Lady to retire completely from public life. November of 1934 saw her helping with the Community Chest Drives in both San Francisco and Los Angeles, following her stipulation that she represent the Girl Scouts.

"Because of her kindly spirit and her never-failing interest in the less-fortunate men and women of the world," explained the chairman of the Woman's Crusade in Los Angeles, "we have asked Mrs. Herbert Hoover to appear in our symposium entitled 'Women Leaders of Today and Tomorrow.'"

"I am glad to be here as a Girl Scout, an active member of that great group of girls who are the women of tomorrow," responded Lou Hoover.

She spoke that day at one of the largest functions of the year. The guests included leaders in women's organizations, civic and professional groups, and members of old and time-honored families who had made the social background of California. She told them the problems facing the Community Chest of Los Angeles were national rather than local ones, owing to the great influx of persons in need. She cited whole families from other parts of the country who had entered the city and ultimately had to be cared for.

"We hear much today about the need of right leadership," she said. "But we need to be good followers, too. Leadership develops with such an attitude and thus our cause is strengthened. It is together we get good things achieved. And we must be wary of would-be leaders who want to destroy our standards."

Both Lou and Bert Hoover were greatly concerned about the subversive influences in the country, which they read about daily in the newspapers. So in May 1935 Bert urged his wife to accept an invitation to appear at the Del Monte meeting of the California Federation of Women's Clubs. There she pointed out the dangers she saw in hiring sensational speakers paid to serve special selfish interests. "They plan organized demoralization, with loss of the people's faith in the integrity of their government and their fellow citizens," she said. Then she quoted Chester Rowell, editor of the *San Francisco Chronicle:*

> Next is Communism, and to it I add the other isms, Fascism, Nazism, and the rest of the evil brood which will flourish in the soil we are preparing—soil impregnated with judicial unfairness, lack of employment opportunities, and lack of protection for old age. This soil is as unAmerican as any of the seeds being sown in it.

Lou Hoover was greatly perturbed by the trend of world events and she spoke from her heart again in a broadcast speech for the Women's Overseas Service League:

> We who stood facing each other across the broken bodies on those army cots, we who know the sound of singing shell and bursting shrapnel, realize now that the war is still on, that it has been going on for thousands of years and will go on for thousands of years to come—the war inside human nature between the helpfulness forces and the selfishness forces.

One public activity from which Lou Hoover most certainly did not wish to retire was the Girl Scout movement. In the fall of that same year, the former First Lady politely declined her first invitation to the White House since she had left it in 1933. In refusing Mrs. Roosevelt's request that she serve as vice-chairman of the Women's Committee on Mobilization for Human Needs, she explained that it would be impossible for her to go to Washington because of her responsibilities at the long-planned Girl Scout National Convention in San Francisco. She wrote: "I feel that the spirit of effective mobilization demands me to be at my post of duty here."

She entered into planning for the San Francisco meeting with enthusiasm and looked forward with pleasure to a reunion with many old friends from the East, among them Mrs. Edgar Rickard, national treasurer. Scouting had always remained close to her heart and now she was free again to engage actively in the program of her favorite character-building agency, which had grown to mammoth proportions in recent years. When the convention of one thousand executives and leaders of the nationwide Scout movement swung into action on October 2, 1935, she was unanimously elected president of the National Girl Scouts Council.

In her acceptance remarks, Mrs. Hoover declared, "The modern Girl Scout may have learned new bits of slang, but fundamental principles have not changed. The Girl Scout of today has a new uniform, but the same courageous heart beats beneath it. She has learned many new mannerisms, but the same character looks out."

After the convention, Lou Hoover traveled East with her husband. She visited the National Scout headquarters in New York as well as Bert's new office, which he had just opened. Together they thoroughly enjoyed the Army-Notre Dame football game at Yankee Stadium.

One month later found the senior Hoovers back in Palo Alto, busily preparing for the trip to Sierra Madre to spend Christmas with Herbert, Peggy, and the children. Peggy's parents, Mr. and Mrs. Douglas Watson of San Francisco, and her young brother Tommy, went with them. The tonneau of the Hoover car was piled high with gifts, which Lou herself had purchased. Allan joined the family for the holidays and they all took in the Rose Bowl football game on New Year's Day.

Herbert was still teaching business economics and aeronautics at California Institute of Technology. Allan worked in a Los Angeles bank and lived at the University Club.

"I am going to move," Allan told his family.

"Where to?" his mother asked.

"Over in the valley, near Bakersfield," he explained, "where I'm investing with several others in the Greenfield Delta Farms. The one at Greenfield covers 2,400 acres and produces alfalfa and cotton. Then there is the Sierra Vista ranch at Chowchilla in Kern County. Our group wants to try out modern methods of agriculture, using big machinery."

"Where do you hire people to do the planting and harvesting?" inquired Douglas Watson.

"We have to hire a lot of migrant labor, but we are also going to build up as much of a permanent population as possible. My most important job will be to oversee the labor camps and make sure that we are providing good living conditions. At Greenfield, we have twenty-five homes, with three to five rooms each. They have thick adobe brick walls, green trim, shingle roofs and cooling devices. The grounds are kept clean, there is hot and cold water, and we provide wood for the stoves."

Lou Hoover exchanged an approving glance with her husband. "Just like your father did for the miners in Burma, Australia, and Russia," she told her son.

After the holiday festivities, Lou Hoover returned to her Girl Scout interests again. Having served in practically every capacity within the Scout movement, she fulfilled with gracious ease the relentless demands upon her as president. While in Duluth, for the Hiawatha Regional convention in May 1936, she was described by a newcomer:

> To me as I watched her work with the leaders and the Scouts at the conference, it seemed she was sweet without

being sugary; competent and able without being arrogant, dominant, or aggressive. She was that rare combination of simplicity and friendliness and quiet dignity that keeps familiarity away. I liked her tremendously.

The new president of the Scouts wore her neat green Girl Scout uniform with pride right through the convention, including the banquet, when most of the women were quite dressed up. This was always her policy in order to give a feeling of all rightness to those women who brought no dinner dresses along.

She exchanged views on modern youth with Mrs. Margaret Culkin Banning, Duluth novelist, before driving on to the town of Virginia, Minnesota, where she wanted to see the new 4-H clubhouse. At Lake Eshquaguma she was entertained by the officers of the St. Louis Country Club, the Farm Bureau Association, and the Federation of 4-H Clubs. Among the welcoming 4-H Club members was Walter Bernstein, who had sent his prize turkey to the Hoovers when they occupied the White House. Lou was shown her thank-you note to Walter, suitably framed and hanging on the wall of the clubhouse reception room. "I did get to meet you," she exclaimed, "even if you didn't come to Washington to see me."

A few days later, Lou Hoover met her husband in Denver to continue the trip home with him by motor. He had just been elected chairman of the Boys Clubs of America.

"I had to do something to try to match you and the Girl Scouts," he told her as they drove over scenic Rocky Mountain roads, captivated by the grandeur of the snow-capped peaks.

They stopped for a day to visit Mr. and Mrs. W. B.

Coberly of Los Angeles, in their mountain ranch summer home, to meet Allan's fiancée, Miss Margaret Coberly. As they sat on the rustic porch in the clear mountain air, Lou Hoover was reminded of the happy days at Camp Rapidan. Soon the young couple arrived on horseback and joined them on the porch. Lou Hoover kissed the pretty girl, whom she liked instantly, and learned with interest that Cobie, as she was called, was a graduate of the University of Southern California, member of Kappa Kappa Gamma, and an active Junior Leaguer. Lou looked at her handsome son and thought, "You have chosen well."

As Lou and Bert Hoover continued their leisurely motor trip, he told her the Boys Clubs of America would aid half a million boys that year through five hundred clubs.

"Well, our own boys are grown," she said, "but we can both enjoy other people's children now."

In July 1936, Lou Hoover went to the San Francisco airport to see her husband off on his sentimental journey to Belgium, invited by the Belgian government and several universities to revisit the scenes of his historic labors in 1919. He wrote to her in detail about the tour of Belgium and his visits to Poland and Germany. He had a happy reunion with Paderewski in Warsaw and a very unhappy meeting with Hitler in Vienna.

While the former President was being honored and feted in Europe, the well-organized smear campaign against him was continuing in the United States. He was pictured by the Democrats in the newspapers as "a monstrous exploiter, a sharp promoter, a hard-headed reactionary, and an enemy of the people." [2]

[2] See *Our Unknown Ex-President,* by Eugene Lyons, pp. 314–334, "Ordeal by Abuse."

Lou Hoover was inwardly distressed by the continuing barrage of assaults upon her husband's character, but in talking it over with Herbert, Jr., she said, "Your father does not try to defend himself against the poison propaganda, but is trying to explain in magazine articles and speeches the philosophy of life which he has been forced by events to symbolize. It is the issue of human liberty and individual initiative versus government controls of both."

"I guess that writing is the best thing to do," replied Herbert. "Did you read Dad's recent article, 'Challenge to Liberty'? He wrote, 'People and governments are blindly wounding, even destroying, those fundamental human liberties which have been the foundation and inspiration of progress since the Middle Ages.'"

"Yes," she replied, "he fears many of the New Deal policies. He recognizes the great need for social reform, but holds an unshakable conviction that relief of distress must remain local and personal rather than to be an impersonal political function. He said that no one with a day's experience in government fails to realize that in all bureaucracies there are three implacable spirits: self-perpetuation, expansion, and an incessant demand for more power."

During the fall months of 1936 in Palo Alto, Lou Hoover was associated with many local activities. On the Woman's Auxiliary Board of the Stanford Convalescent Home she aided money-raising undertakings for the benefit of the chronically ill children in the home.

At Stanford, she worked actively to organize "The Friends of Music" to insure musical concerts for the community. She invited leaders in music circles to her hospitable home to meet Mrs. Elizabeth Sprague Coolidge, Stanford's original benefactor of chamber music. Under the direction of Lou Hoover and Warren D. Allen, director of Stanford's Music Division, the Friends of Music secured many outstanding music events for the university, often because the former First Lady had so many friends among the musicians of the East Coast and abroad.

As Christmas approached, Herbert Hoover longed for deep-sea fishing accepted the invitation of George Getz to use his yacht, *Virago*, as headquarters. Lou and Bert Hoover flew to Miami Beach and spent the holidays fishing in the Gulf Stream.

On January 27, 1937, Mr. and Mrs. W. B. Coberly formally announced the engagement of their daughter, Margaret, to Allan Hoover, and in February the two families met in Phoenix, Arizona, to spend a few days together. Afterward, Allan went East with his father by train and Lou Hoover enjoyed driving back to Los Angeles with the charming, zestful Cobie. The wedding date had been set for March 17.

It was with excited and pleasurable anticipation that Lou and Bert drove to Los Angeles to join about one hundred guests who were invited to the Coberly home for the wedding. The groom's devoted mother was aware of the delicate beauty of a flowering peach tree outside, framed in the large plate-glass window, as Allan followed the Reverend Dr. D. Charles Gardner, chaplain emeritus of Stanford, into the living room.

Following the wedding ceremony, the newlyweds flew to Nassau in the Bahamas for their honeymoon and the senior Hoovers went to New York. When the honeymooners returned on April 16, the two couples met again in Des Moines, Iowa, and drove to West Branch, where they talked about the plan to restore the Hoover homestead there and turn it over to the Iowa Historical Society.

Back home in California, Lou Hoover remained very

active with the local Girl Scouts. She helped to launch the annual Girl Scout financial drive in Palo Alto in the spring of 1937. Also, as national president, she traveled to Savannah, Georgia, the first meeting place of the charter members of the Scouts, for their Silver Jubilee.

"Our girls, out of all proportion to their age, their experience or their numbers, are exerting their influence on our country," she said in her talk. "The old order changes. The whole world has been changing its ways as it does during every quarter century. We hope we have been keeping pace with it in ways that are good. We hope we have seen some of its more general mistakes and have avoided them."

During the 1937 convention, Lou Hoover unveiled a bronze memorial tablet dedicated to Juliette Low, in the headquarters building, which was the converted stable of the Low home, given by the founder to the Girl Scouts. In her remarks, Lou said, "This building has housed Girl Scout activities for a full quarter of a century, during which the organization has grown from the original group of twelve to a nationwide movement with a membership of 400,000."

She was an interested and amused spectator when twelve girls, representing the original Girl Scouts, re-enacted the first meeting in 1912. They all wore the dark shirtwaists, bloomers, and large hair ribbons of the 1912 period, did dumbbell exercises, and played games that were the vogue when the movement began.

On November 23, there was a gathering of the Hoover families in Los Angeles for Thanksgiving and the football game. At that time plans were laid for all to come to Palo Alto for Christmas.

Lou made many holiday plans for the grandchildren and replenished the supply of toys. Allan and Cobie drove up from Bakersfield, and Herbert and his family came from Sierra Madre. Christmas Day was devoted to the grandchildren, but the following day the adults went to see the preview of a Paramount movie dramatizing Herbert Hoover's relief work in Belgium.

In June 1938, the wife of the former President was an enthusiastic guest at the Herbert Hoover Junior High School out-of-door graduation pageant in San Jose. "Now, when I was graduating from grammar school forty years ago," she told them, "things looked uncertain, too. But youth found a place in the world, just as it had always done and always will, and the youth of today is better prepared to face a more complicated situation."

A few weeks later, she examined with interest the architect's drawings for the Lou Henry Hoover School in Whittier, named for herself.

Lou Hoover's constant interest in university affairs, plus her genuine concern for a sound program of sports and athletics for girls, made her a frequent visitor to the Women's Gymnasium at Stanford. She discussed problems of athletics, health, and recreation with the director of the Women Students' Health Service,[3] and they also compared their China experiences. Together they tried to plan new curriculum opportunities for the Stanford girls, both in sports and in professional physical-education courses for teachers. They debated to what extent girls should be encouraged to participate in the more strenuous and highly competitive forms of athletics and agreed that solution of this problem should depend upon the ability to measure the effects on the nervous systems and physiology of the participants.

They discussed details of minimum physical-fitness stan-

[3] The director was Dr. Helen B. Pryor, author of this book, *Lou Henry Hoover, Gallant First Lady*.

dards. Mrs. Hoover, an ardent exponent of out-of-door living, believed that wise compulsory physical-education activities would raise the physical-fitness levels of the college girls. She was particulary concerned about physical fitness for women because of the gathering war clouds in Europe. During the school year 1938–1939 she was worried about Germany's annexation of Austria and Czechoslovakia, and Italy's penetration of Albania. "If war comes again," she said, "these girls must be trained to contribute real service to their country." When consulted by Dr. Pryor about the possibility of developing a curriculum in physical therapy, she was genuinely interested and enthusiastic and heartily endorsed the idea. She immediately commented, "The importance of well-trained physiotherapists in all kinds of physical rehabilitation is obvious, and I think that for women students it offers a field as important as nursing."

The war clouds continued to gather and one day Herbert Hoover said to his wife, "It looks as if another war is inevitable and we will be needed to help with relief once more. Many of my activities are centered in New York and since I have already set up an office there, if war comes, shall we leave Palo Alto again?"

"Yes, of course, we will have to go," she replied, and her outward calm gave her husband no clue of the inner pang she felt.

The senior Hoovers welcomed Allan and Cobie when they moved to Palo Alto at this time, having decided that since Allan had to travel around so much on ranch business Palo Alto would be just as good for headquarters as Bakersfield or Fresno. Mrs. Hoover helped them to find a house on Fulton Street.

Worry over the war situation vanished temporarily from Lou Hoover's mind when Allan Henry Hoover was born on November 15, 1938. She went to the Palo Alto Hospital every day to see Cobie and the baby and then spent as much time as she could with her newest grandchild in the Fulton Street home.

In the meanwhile, Herbert Hoover spent more and more time in New York, as the major aggressions in Europe occurred, and his understanding wife knew that it would be only a matter of weeks until they would have to live in that Eastern metropolis.

XVI

BACK TO NEW YORK

•

1940–1944

In palo alto, late in 1939, Lou and Bert Hoover read about the partition of Poland by Germany and Russia and the invasion of Finland by Russia, and wondered who would be the next victims. Before many months passed, news came that Denmark and Norway and finally Holland and Belgium were overrun by German armies. Lou Hoover remembered with a heavy heart the devastation she had witnessed twenty-five years before, during World War I, in those same countries. With this crisis in world affairs, she knew the United States government officials would be calling on her husband for help, since his experience in these countries would be invaluable.

When the call came, she completely approved of his heading up the national Finnish Relief Fund, with headquarters at 420 Lexington Avenue, New York. "Here we are sixty-six years old," she told him; "we have been deeply involved in one war and in relief work. I guess we will know how to do it all over again after twenty-five years."

With a stout heart, she started packing their things, and

233

said good-by to her many California friends and to her garden. Once again she pulled up roots in her beloved Palo Alto, and this time transplanted her life with that of her husband, as always, to the Towers at the Waldorf-Astoria Hotel, thirty floors above Park Avenue in New York City.

"We will use four rooms for Bert's office headquarters," Mrs. Hoover told Dr. W. P. Lucas, an old C.R.B.[1] friend who came to visit. She introduced two secretaries, who were busy at typewriters in the outer room. "His private office is this adjoining room and he uses that large table for his desk. He set it diagonally across a corner of the room, flanked by windows, so that he can look out on the surrounding skyscrapers. On top of the desk-table is his telephone, a buzzer, and always stacks of papers."

"Looks like the Chief," commented the visitor.

"Our living quarters are on this floor, too," continued Lou Hoover, "but not connected directly with the office space. We are very comfortably situated."

"I am glad you are close by," was the reply, "because the Chief never allowed himself either time or thought for a personal existence, but kept himself constantly subjected to duty."

Dr. Lucas later described seeing Herbert Hoover that day. "His gray hair is thinning, his high forehead tends to obscure his eyes, which look tired, and his voice sounds a bit husky. His clothes reflect a bygone era, stiff collar, high black shoes, plain dark suit, and somber tie. As he posed for an artist this week, he requested, 'Don't make it too evident that I need a haircut, lest Mrs. Hoover twit me for not taking time to get to a barbershop.' He is still uneasy with strangers and talks with self-conscious for-

[1] Commission for Relief in Belgium.

mality when being interviewed. But he loosened up with me."

Lou and Bert Hoover kept Palo Alto as their legal residence and commuted frequently between their homes there and in New York.

She swung into the old spirit of the relief work that spring when she accompanied her husband to a benefit luncheon for the Finnish Relief Fund and sat with Countess Eva Sparre, sister of Field Marshal Baron Karl Gustav Mannerheim of Finland. She heard Mayor F. H. LaGuardia tell the 950 guests that they could give money for arms as well as for civilian relief.

"I don't know if that is in keeping with diplomatic usage," said the mayor, "but I know the invasion of Finland is not in keeping with diplomatic usage. Democracy is on the side of Finland, civilization is on the side of Finland, and Finland is on the side of both."

When Herbert Hoover spoke, his wife nodded in vigorous agreement. "Every line of the dispatches from Finland raises the emotions of every American," he said. "Finland has become a symbol of stanch men and women fighting to preserve their liberties at any cost. It is a struggle we have seen but few times in history."

Lou Hoover was proud when her husband's efforts had helped to raise more than a million dollars for Finnish relief during the first month of the campaign. She assisted him as he launched the Polish and Belgian relief organizations. Later, after other groups had organized Dutch and Norwegian relief committees, Herbert Hoover became head of the combined effort, the national committee working to provide food for the five small democracies. Lou Hoover slid easily into her former patterns of securing relief funds.

Although her days were full of relief work, she still

maintained her active interest in Scouting and attended many Girl Scout meetings. She firmly believed that peace must be built in the young people. Clad in the simple green uniform of the Girl Scouts, Lou Hoover, as honorary vice president of the national organization, summed up her many years of Scouting activity with a lesson drawn from the new war in Europe.

"With all the national and international evils loose in the world, homemakers are the real peacemakers," she told her intent audience at the twenty-seventh annual convention in Philadelphia. "As we look across the ocean and see the turmoil in other lands and realize what we have to do with our citizens to preserve our ideals, the full value of the Girl Scout movement is brought home to us."

Reporters wanted her to discuss American neutrality and asked her if she thought American youth, through such organizations as the Girl Scouts, could do anything to keep the United States at peace.

"The Girl Scouts can do exactly what any other group of citizens can do," she replied. "That is, teach restraint and tolerance and interest its members in the discovery of truth and in remaining emotionally balanced."

She related that refugee Girl Scouts from Europe had been taken into American Girl Scout organizations as soon as they arrived in the United States. "In Germany, Italy, and Russia," she recounted, "the Girl Scouts were discontinued by the local governments. As they began having difficult times, Scouts from other countries assisted them by sending clothing and money."

She explained that the Girl Scouts of America were helping Scouts in England and France, but were unable to reach the girls in the subjugated countries. "The Girl

Scout program grows increasingly important through the years," she insisted.

Lou Hoover followed the war news avidly, as the British and French armies were extracted from Dunkirk and when Hitler finally attacked Russia. She was glad when Churchill took over as Prime Minister and ordered the children sent out of London and every citizen to enroll in defense. She vividly remembered 1914 in London and approved of President Roosevelt's policy to send arms to England and France.

We will be needed in relief work for a long time yet, she thought.

However, her family always came first in her interests and she wanted to be with Bert for his sixty-sixth birthday, on August 10, 1940. He was making key addresses for the GOP around the country, so Allan and Lou joined him for a trout-fishing trip up the West Yellowstone River on his birthday. Two days later, they went with him to Colorado Springs.

From the Colorado meeting they all went to Palo Alto, arriving just in time for the funeral on September 3 of Mildred Brooke Hoover, writer on California history and wife of Theodore, who was now emeritus dean of Stanford's School of Mining Engineering.

That fall, Lou Hoover was elected chairman of the Western Women's Committee assisting the Salvation Army in its campaign for clothing for one million war refugees in Europe. In October, she received a special appeal from Generosity Warehouse in London, and signed by the Queen, requesting clothes for persons outside the areas controlled by the Nazis. Mrs. Hoover sent out a call through the schools, asking the children to bring in clothing.

"This can be character-building work for our children,"

she said, "when they respond and begin to think about other children in distress in Europe." She assisted volunteers from the Parent-Teacher Association, who sorted and graded the garments and packed them at the Salvation Army headquarters in San Francisco.

Early in November, Mrs. Coberly came to Palo Alto from Los Angeles. On November 9, 1940, both grandmothers were excited and pleased when baby Andrew, son of Cobie and Allan Hoover, weighed in at the Palo Alto Hospital at eight pounds, ten ounces. Lou Hoover announced, "I'm going to send a telegram to Bert from Allan Henry, telling his grandpa that he has a baby brother."

She attended Girl Scout conferences throughout the United States whenever she could get away from her many activities in New York. She discussed the peacetime program of the Scouts at a Northwest Regional Conference in Seattle, early in May 1941:

> It is just as necessary in peacetime to build a good strong country as it is to stop and protect it against the threat of war. The emphasis in Scouting is always on the need for good homes and good communities and the part that Girl Scouts can play in helping to build them. Also, the Scout organization is not going to adopt a national unified defense program because conditions over the nation are so different.

From Seattle, Lou Hoover went to Palo Alto, where she enjoyed a few weeks at her campus home, highlighted by three university events: Stanford's fiftieth anniversary, an honorary degree for her, and the opening of the new Hoover War Library.

Although she had received seven honorary degrees in the past few years, none meant so much to her as the one from her Alma Mater. For the commencement ceremony on June 12, she again donned academic cap and gown. Two representatives, a man and a woman, from each of the graduating classes marched in the commencement procession as a symbol of the university's anniversary. Lou Henry Hoover, representing the class of 1898, marched with Charles A. Beardsley, class of 1906, because both were to be commencement speakers. The Sunday-afternoon sun was bright and warm and Lou Hoover was appreciative of the lovely trees at the back of the stage in the Laurence Frost Amphitheater as she faced the 723 students in the graduating class and their proud relatives massed on the grassy terraces beyond the faculty. At the conclusion of her talk, she was awarded an honorary fellowship from Stanford. "It gives me a warm feeling around my heart to receive this recognition from the school I have loved for so many years," she said. She carried her new diploma [2] with dignity as she left the amphitheater and guarded it lovingly until it was safely home.

Next week, the tower will be dedicated, she thought in happy anticipation, as she passed it on her way home. Since World War I, when Herbert Hoover had started his collection with project Pack Rat, the flow of historical materials into the Hoover War Library at Stanford had been so tremendous that a new building was needed to house them. Millions of documents and books made this unique collection a center for advanced study and research on the causes of war and on problems of political, social, and economic change during the twentieth century. Over the years, Mr. Hoover, with the help of many of his friends, had raised most of the $750,000 needed to build the new library.

[2] It is now on display in the Lou Henry Hoover Memorial room at the Hoover Institution, along with her original diploma.

Herbert Hoover arrived from New York in time for the dedication of the towering landmark, which was to be the new home of the Hoover War Library. He and his wife rode the elevator to the top of the 285-foot tower on the fourteenth floor and went onto the observation platform to enjoy the panoramic views of the Stanford University and the Mid-Peninsula.

Lou Hoover was especially fascinated by watching the installation of the Belgian carillon here. The thirty-five-bell carillon was presented to Stanford University by the Belgian American Educational Foundation, in gratitude for Mr. Hoover's famine relief services during World War I.

"Mr. Kamiel LeFevere, carillonneur of the Riverside Church in New York City, placed the clavier or keyboard with great care," explained Lou Hoover. "The bells of this carillon are called 'silvery bells' because of their beautiful tone and exquisite harmonics."

Many momentos of Herbert Hoover's long and active career were placed on exhibition in the first-floor rotunda. In a room across the hall, named the Lou Henry Hoover room, many valuable objects of art collected by Mrs. Hoover, as well as records of her contributions to peace and humanitarian movements, were displayed.

In his dedication address on June 20, Herbert Hoover said:

The purpose of the Hoover Institution is to promote peace. In addition to the War Library there is a place for the staff and cooperating scholars to carry on research. Here will be found the raw materials of history in the making. These are the documents which record the suffering, the self-denial, the devotion, the heroic deeds of men. Surely from these records there can be help to mankind in its confusions and perplexities and its yearning for peace. Its records stand as a challenge to those who promote war.

The Hoovers spent the summer at their California home. On October 2, Lou Hoover arranged a buffet luncheon for the members of the class of 1895, Bert's class, and the first one to spend four years at Stanford. As a special honor, President Ray Lyman Wilbur was "promoted" from the class of 1896 to 1895 so that he might attend the reunion. Mrs. David Starr Jordan, wife of the first president of the university and her daughter Edith Jordan Gardner of Berkeley were among the guests. Following the luncheon, the Stanford pioneers with their wives and friends gathered on the terrace where they could enjoy looking at the valley and the bay over their coffee as they reminisced about the old days at Stanford and their former classmates. They laid plans for a fiftieth-year anniversary celebration for their class in 1945.

The senior Hoovers were back in New York before the attack on Pearl Harbor, December 7, 1941, when the United States was plunged into the war. Lou Hoover was stunned by the rapid series of disasters. Following the destruction of the main Pacific fleet in Hawaii, the Japanese also destroyed the United States Air Force at Manila. She asked her husband, "How is it possible, how could they have done this?"

"All we know is that they did do it," he answered, "but an analytical investigation is under way."

Lou saw a ray of hope in the war-blackened sky when she and her husband went to Washington, D. C., to attend the meeting of the League of Nations' representatives on January 2, 1942. The Geneva League was dissolved and a new organization called the United Nations was set up tentatively by twenty-six nations, opposed to the fascist coalition of Germany, Japan, and Italy with their satellites. The member nations organized to promote world peace and security. They worked out a plan to keep the best parts of the old organization intact and to assure continuance of all essential work. The Labor section of the Geneva League was re-established in Montreal, Health in Washington, D. C., Economics in Princeton, New Jersey, and the ownership of the buildings and library at Geneva was transferred to the United Nations.

"At least there is a first structure for keeping peace," exulted Lou Hoover.

"In its infancy, with a lot of growing up to do," was her husband's comment.

After Pearl Harbor, World War II moved on swiftly and relentlessly with the invasion of the Philippines, Malay, and Singapore by Japan.

More and more of Mrs. Hoover's time was now spent in the New York apartment, as the war demands became increasingly heavy. She received clothing made by school children in response to an appeal for the air-raid victims. "Generosity Warehouse" was stocked with clothing and comforts for women and children dispossessed by the bombings. In a familiar role, she spent many hours directing volunteers and in preparing clothing and supplies for these homeless refugees, with whom she could identify so easily because of her London war work during World War I.

She also gave many hours of work to the Red Cross, preparing supplies to be sent to American boys on overseas duty. Heartbreaking stories from across both the Atlantic and the Pacific oceans came into the Red Cross headquarters daily.

When Rangoon fell and the British were driven out of

Burma, she thought about the years of her early married life when she had fought mosquitoes and devised other methods to keep her sons free from the health dangers of that jungle country.

The war moved closer to home as she read about the United States troops attacking the Japanese at Guadalcanal. Finally, the turning point came with the battle of Midway in June, and Lou Hoover felt a little lessening of the war tension but she was aware of her own physical weariness.

On their way home to Palo Alto in the summer of 1942, Lou and Bert Hoover stopped off to check progress on the restoration of the Hoover birthplace at West Branch, Iowa. "The landscaping has been done very well," she remarked as their car approached the simple house on Wapsinonoc Creek, which Eli and Jesse Hoover had built in 1870. "The pine trees, maples, and willows along the bank of the creek make a nice green background for the house. The tulips and peonies create a colorful splash and the rose garden is coming along."

"Yes," he replied, "and the outside of the cottage now looks as it did originally. Allan is doing a really good job supervising the reconstruction."

"Allan paid you a nice tribute, dear, when he bought this place to preserve it for its historic value, but only you can supply the information needed to make authentic changes. And he has built an attractive house for the caretakers."

They found the inside of the house also restored to look as it did when Jesse and Hulda Hoover made it their first home. The structure, 14 by 20 feet, was divided into two rooms. There was a bedroom containing a walnut dresser, a washstand with china pitcher and bowl, a rope bed with a fat straw tick and comfortable feather mattress, snowy linen sheets and a hand-pieced quilt and bolster pillow. The other room was the living room and kitchen combined. It was equipped with chairs and a table, a wood-burning stove, and a pump that brought water into a zinc-lined sink. Herbert Hoover was consulted about the items of furniture.

Later, the senior Hoovers had a pleasant leisurely stay in Palo Alto and Herbert Hoover attended the Bohemian Grove encampment up Russian River, where he was honored by the officers of the Bohemian Club before the couple returned to New York in the fall.

There was less need now for volunteers to work at the Red Cross headquarters or to collect clothing for European war refugees, so Lou Hoover gradually lightened her load. She went to the theater, read books that interested her, and enjoyed many musical events.

On January 9, 1943, a telegram came to the Waldorf Towers apartment announcing that Allan and Cobie had a little daughter born that day in Palo Alto and that they had named her Lou Henry.

The baby's grandfather, with a pleased smile, advised, "You had better be off to see your namesake."

"As if I needed urging," was the reply. "My bag is all packed."

While Lou Hoover was in Palo Alto, she attended an interesting half-century celebration on the campus. She was an honor guest along with Mrs. Ray Lyman Wilbur, Mrs. John Caspar Branner, and Mrs. David Starr Jordan of the Stanford YWCA, for the fiftieth anniversary celebration of that organization.

Back in New York, an insidious physical and mental fatigue began to take its toll on Mrs. Hoover, although she thought herself to be in good health. When she con-

sulted her personal physician, Dr. Ralph Boots, he limited
her activity.

On January 7, 1944, Lou Hoover attended a concert
with friends in the afternoon and returned to the Waldorf
Towers to rest briefly before going out for dinner with her
husband. She told him she was very tired when she went
to her bedroom to lie down, but there was no other complaint. About seven o'clock she was stricken with a sudden
acute heart attack. Mr. Hoover summoned Dr. Boots, who
came immediately, but he was unable to save her and she
died within a few minutes. Herbert and Allan flew to
New York immediately to be with their father.

On January 9, the Reverend Dr. George Paul Sargent,
rector of St. Bartholomew's Church in New York City,
conducted a simple funeral service, following the Episcopal Book of Common Prayer. This was attended by one
thousand persons, many of them prominent in political
and business life. At Lou Hoover's earlier request, there
was no eulogy. Dr. Sargent was assisted by Rufus Jones,
chairman of the American Friends Service Committee.
The vested choir of the church participated, singing Mrs.
Hoover's favorite hymn, "Nearer, My God, to Thee."

Mrs. Hoover had never become a member of the Friends
Meeting, although she believed very sincerely in their
principles as exemplified by her husband. Nevertheless,
she herself remained an Episcopalian.

The casket was placed in the chancel of the church,
covered with white roses, sweet peas, and a cross of
lilies, while on each side of the chancel were arranged
hundreds of floral offerings. Seated to the left of the
casket was Herbert Hoover, flanked by Herbert and Allan.
Among the mourners were two hundred Girl Scouts in a
delegation headed by Mrs. Valentine E. Macy, Dr. Lillian
Gilbreth, and Mrs. Paul Kammer, members of the board of

directors. The casket was later sent by train to Palo Alto, accompanied by Herbert Hoover and his two sons. They were met by Peggy, Cobie, and the six grandchildren and were soon surrounded by hosts of greatly saddened relatives and friends.

On January 14, the Palo Alto business firms voluntarily closed during the time of the memorial service for Lou Henry Hoover, and the flag on the Veterans' Building was at half mast all day in tribute to her memory.

Chancellor Ray Lyman Wilbur, a friend of Lou Henry Hoover since her college days, paid tribute to her at the memorial service held on Friday afternoon at 4:30 P.M. in Stanford's Memorial Church. He characterized her as "a fine friendly American woman who will be remembered as a successful wife and mother."

He continued:

Complimentary things are usually said about noted people when they die. It is significant that all these things were said of Mrs. Hoover while she lived. She was recognized during her lifetime as a uniquely intelligent woman, who refused to let official formalities interfere with her deep and friendly interest in people. The place where the Hoover family lived, whether in California or China or the White House, was never a house or a mansion. It was, because of Mrs. Hoover, a home.

The ceremony, in charge of Dr. D. Elton Trueblood, Stanford University chaplain and a Quaker, was a very simple one. There was music by Elizabeth Pierce Kincade, violinist, and the university choir. Five hundred Girl Scouts from Palo Alto, Redwood City, Los Altos, Menlo Park, San Mateo, and Burlingame attended in a body with their leaders.

For fifteen minutes following the memorial service the

carillon in the Hoover Tower sent out notes of sacred music. Only members of the immediate family attended the burial rites and said good-by to Lou Henry Hoover in the beautiful Alta Mesa cemetery on the edge of Palo Alto.

The Girl Scouts, complying with the request that no flowers be sent, established a national fund in memory of their devoted and tireless leader.

Hundreds of editorials and magazine articles eulogizing Lou Henry Hoover appeared throughout the United States and abroad at the time of her death. A few quotations will serve to show in what high esteem she was held.

Scimitar, Memphis, Tennessee: The death of Mrs. Herbert Hoover will inspire sympathy for the former President in the heart of every American who recalls how graciously, yet unostentatiously, she presided over the White House. A woman of fine gentility and intelligence, Mrs. Hoover was essentially a homemaker whose chief desire in life was to ease, in so far as it lay within her womanly power, the vast and varied burdens which the former President assumed during his long public career. One of Mrs. Hoover's chief characteristics was her ability to be of great aid to her husband, yet remain completely in the background.

New York Times, New York City: Mrs. Hoover could have had a distinguished career in any walk of life. As it was, it fell to her to distinguish herself where the standards of attainment are necessarily high, as wife of a cabinet member and later as First Lady of the land. It was characteristic of her that her charm and talents did not depend upon, but rather enhanced, whatever circumstances she found in which to exert them.

Chronicle, San Francisco, California: In her unobtrusive way, Mrs. Herbert Hoover was all her life a force for human betterment. The one instance in which she came into public prominence she never sought, her leadership of the Girl Scouts of America, is slight measure of her widespread but unpublicized activity in all manner of works for young people. She is mourned by a multitude of friends who had reason to love her.

Will Irwin in *The American Girl,* the Girl Scout magazine:

> She kept up her scholarly interests all her life. When she broke into the conversation, whether it was on the mining business or American politics or Chinese history, she knew what she was talking about. Tolerant of human frailties, she did not tolerate them in herself. She was almost too kind. The people whom she helped over the hard places with money, with sympathy, and with counsel must have run into the thousands. Never, even in the darkest days of the depression which hung over the White House like a cloud, did she give any sign of waning courage. She died the youngest woman of her years I have ever known.

> *Palo Alto Times, Palo Alto, California:* As long as Americans cherish honest work, neighborliness, truth, integrity, courage, and democracy, Lou Henry Hoover's essential spirit will live. She has not said good-by.

Following Mrs. Hoover's wishes, the Hoover campus home was presented to Stanford University to be used as the home of the president. She had stipulated that in return, for a period of six years, the university should present an annual gift of $10,000 to the Hoover Institution of War, Revolution and Peace. This money was to be used "in research and the publication of documents advancing peace in the world."

This stipulation was symbolic of her marriage role. Mrs. Hoover was a full partner with her husband but always put his interests first and was content to remain in the background. However, all her life she was a person in her own right, one who was very human, who enjoyed informality, and was never impressed with her own importance.

Her friends will always remember her as the gracious hostess genuinely interested in every guest, who never spoke harshly of anyone or condemned another human being. A gentle, friendly woman, she never sat in judgment of anyone's conduct but her own. She often spoke out vigorously against something that had been said but never against the person who said it. She left an imprint of progressiveness combined with kindly tolerance on her world.

ADDENDA

Shortly after the death of Herbert Hoover on October 20, 1964, the remains of his wife were moved from Alta Mesa cemetery to West Branch, Iowa, to share his burial place there.

Lou Henry Hoover's life inspired many memorials and two of the recent ones are in her beloved home town of Palo Alto and on the Stanford campus.

The Lou Henry Hoover Memorial Building, which houses the Mid-Peninsula Young Women's Christian Association, at 4161 Alma Street, Palo Alto, was dedicated April 28, 1963. It serves the communities of Palo Alto, Los Altos, and Mountain View.

The Lou Henry Hoover Building, which adjoins the Hoover Tower on the Stanford campus, was dedicated on October 9, 1967. It provides additional space for the expanding Hoover Institution, and especially for the research program in national and international affairs. It houses the great Chinese and Japanese collections, which represent unique holdings of books, magazines, and newspapers. The Oriental décor of the lobby area leading to the East Asian collections is enhanced by Chinese art objects. An underground passage connects the new building with the Hoover Tower.

APPENDIX

1. Lou Henry Hoover—Family Tree

Father's family:
Great Grandfather, William Henry, born 1776, married Abigail Hunt.
Grandfather, William Henry, Jr., born 1809, married Mary Dwire.
Father, Charles Delano Henry, 1844-1929, married Florence Weed.
   Charles' brothers: William D. and Addis M. Henry.

Mother's family:
Grandfather, Joshua Weed.
Father, Phineas Weed, born 1823, married Mary Scobey.
   Their children: Janey, Wallace and Florence Weed.

Charles Delano Henry married Florence Weed, June 17, 1873.

2. One of Lou Henry's early oil paintings of wild flowers is hanging in the teen-age lounge in the Lou Henry Hoover Memorial Building of the Mid-Peninsula YWCA in Palo Alto, California. This picture was presented by Mr. Kosta Boris, a family friend.

3. In California, a private University, a memorial to Leland Stanford, Jr., had been organized in Palo Alto by a man who

had little formal education but great respect for learning. Leland and Jane Lathrop Stanford laid the foundation of the Stanford fortune by opening a country store in Sacramento and gradually acquiring land. Ambitious young Stanford studied law at night and went into politics. Elected Governor of California in January 1862, while Abraham Lincoln was in the White House, he was determined to keep his state in the Union and against slavery. He invested in the fabulously successful Lincoln mine near Colombia in California's Mother Lode country.

After eighteen childless years, the Stanfords had a son and their lives began to revolve around Leland Junior. The Stanfords, who had 8,000 acres in Santa Clara Valley, developed a beautiful summer home on the farm near Palo Alto.

To further their son's education, his parents took young Leland to Europe when he was fifteen. Typhoid infection acquired in Athens proved fatal to the boy. He died in Florence, Italy, on March 13, 1884. After they lost their beloved son, the Stanford's enormous fortune held no value for them. In lieu of grandchildren, Mr. and Mrs. Stanford quite naturally decided to establish a University "of high degree" to carry on the name of their son. His school, they decided, must be a practical one where students were taught that labor is respectable and honorable.

4. Honorary degrees received by Lou Henry Hoover.

Mills College, California	Master of Arts	May 14, 1923
Whittier College, California	Doctor of Literature	August 17, 1928
Swarthmore College, Pennsylvania	Doctor of Litterarum	June 3, 1929
Elmira College, New York	Legum Doctoris	June 9, 1930
Goucher College, Maryland	Doctor of Laws	April 24, 1931

College of Wooster, Massachusetts	Doctor Litterarum Humanorum	May 14, 1932
Tufts College, Massachusetts	Magistri in Artibus	June 13, 1932
Stanford University, California	Fellowship	June 20, 1941

5. Lou Hoover and Miss Lida Hafford, Executive Secretary of the General Federation of Women's Clubs, took the lead in the work of the newly formed Women's National Law Enforcement League. Mrs. Edward Franklin White was elected national chairman; Mrs. Henry W. Peabody, chairman of the executive committee; and Lou Hoover, chairman of the Washington Chapter. Active co-operation came from most of the women's organizations in the country, including the Young Women's Christian Association, National Council of Women, Congress of Mothers, Parent-Teacher Association, American Legion Auxiliary, Women's Christian Temperance Union, League of Women Voters, women's church organizations representing scores of clubs of women in all walks of life. These and others of the most prominent women in the country, socially, politically and financially, were behind the movement to promote respect for law.

6. Mrs. Mabel Willebrandt, Assistant Attorney General, and Mrs. John D. Rockefeller, Jr., were among the speakers. Mrs. Willebrandt said, "Corruption in high places is revolting but the condition that will prove fatal to this country is lethargy. Whole communities have civic sleeping-sickness all over the land."

Mrs. Rockefeller, representing the National Board of the YWCA, said, "Our whole future is at stake if our children see their parents scornfully choose laws of the land they will obey and those which they will ignore. I am deeply concerned with the welfare of the girlhood of this country and deplore the present laxity."

The Pen Women's League stressed the idea that obedience to law should be written into school text books. Lou Hoover summed up with "Bad men are elected by good women who stay away from the polls on election day."

BIBLIOGRAPHY

BOOKS

Beard, Charles A. and Mary. *New Basic History of the United States*. New York. Doubleday & Co., 1960.

Bliven, Bruce. *World Changers*. New York. John Day Co., 1967.

Cunnington, C. Willett. *English Women's Clothing in the Nineteenth Century*. London. Faber and Faber, 1937.

Elliott, Orrin Leslie. *Stanford University, The First Twenty-five Years*. Stanford. Stanford Press, 1937.

Hinshaw, David. *Herbert Hoover: American Quaker*. New York. Farrar Co., 1950.

Hoover, Herbert. *Memoirs*. Vol. 1, Years of Adventure 1874–1920. New York. Macmillan, 1951.

————. *Memoirs*. Vol. 2, The Cabinet and the Presidency 1920–1933. New York. Macmillan, 1952.

Kellogg, Vernon. *Herbert Hoover*. New York. Appleton, 1920.

Lyons, Eugene. *Our Unknown President: A Portrait of Herbert Hoover*. New York. Doubleday & Co., 1950.

Mackey, Margaret Gilbert, and Louise Pinckney Sooy. *Early California Costumes*. Stanford. Stanford Press, 1932.

McGee, Dorothy Horton. *Herbert Hoover: Engineer, Humanitarian, Statesman*. New York. Dodd Mead & Co., 1959, Revised edition 1965.

Mirrielees, Edith R. *Stanford, The Story of a University*. New York. Putnam, 1959.

Miller, William. *A History of the United States.* New York. George Brazillen, 1958.

Nevins, Allan, and Henry S. Commager. *A Short History of the United States.* New York. Random House, 1956.

Rogers, Agnes. *Women Are Here To Stay.* New York. Harper Brothers, 1949.

Wells, H. G. *Outline of History.* Garden City. Doubleday & Co., Garden City Books, 1956.

MAGAZINES

Black, Ruby. "The White House Day," *Household Magazine,* February, 1930.

Brigham, Reuben. "At the National 4H Camp," *National 4H Club Magazine,* 1930.

Caldwell, Mrs. W. W. "Mrs. Herbert Hoover," *The Spokane Woman,* April 12, 1928.

Canfield, Dorothy. "A Good Girl Scout," *Good Housekeeping,* April, 1930.

Collins, Frederick K. "Mrs. Hoover in the White House," *Woman's Home Companion,* April, 1928.

Dyer, Susan L. "Friends of Music at Stanford," *Alumni Magazine,* 1951.

Englund, Amy Jane. "Mrs. Hoover—Homemaker and World Citizen," *Better Homes and Gardens,* April, 1929.

Frazer, Elizabeth. "Mrs. Herbert Hoover," *Saturday Evening Post,* June 9, 1928.

Hall, Mildred. Article in the Business and Professional Women's Magazine, 1928.

Hard, Anne. "Mrs. Hoover—Friendly Impressions," *Woman Citizen,* October, 1926.

Harmond, Dudley. "Dining with the Hoovers—What a Guest Eats at the Table of the Food Administrator," *Ladies Home Journal,* March, 1918.

Hinshaw, Augusta. "How the Hoovers Brought Up Their Boys," *Parents Magazine,* December, 1929.

Irwin, Will. "Lou Henry Hoover, an Appreciation by Will Irwin," *The American Girl,* March, 1944.

Kellogg, Charlotte. "Mrs. Hoover," *Ladies Home Journal,* September, 1930.

———. "What is Mrs. Hoover Like?" *Woman's Home Companion,* June, 1920.

———. "The Young Hoovers," *Saturday Evening Post,* March 2, 1929.

Keyes, Frances Parkinson. "The Ladies in the Case," *Delineator,* March, 1928.

Lane, Rose Wilder. "The Making of Herbert Hoover," *Sunset,* Vol. 44, 1920.

Mesta, Perle. "First Ladies I Have Known," *McCalls Magazine,* March, 1963.

Norris, Kathleen. "A Woman Looks at Hoover," *Colliers,* May 5, 1926.

Palmer, Frederick. "Mrs. Hoover Knows," *Ladies Home Journal,* March, 1929.

Post, Emily Price. "First Lady of the Land," *Cosmopolitan,* October, 1932.

Raleigh, Walter. "The Adventurous-Home-Loving Mrs. Hoover, Future First Lady," *California Christian Advocate,* February 28, 1929.

———. "When Mrs. Hoover was a Girl," *Christian Endeavor World,* June, 1929.

Rinehart, Mary Roberts. "A New First Lady Becomes Hostess for the Nation," *World's Work,* March, 1929.

Sangster, Margaret E. "Mrs. Hoover—Herself," *Christian Herald,* October 6, 1928.

St. John, Adela Rogers. "Mrs. Herbert Hoover," *Liberty,* October 20, 1928.

Vandenberg, Hazel Whitaker. "Just Being the Wife of Our President," *Everygirls*—The Magazine of the Campfire Girls, September, 1929.

Smith, Nioxala Greeley. "Wives of Famous Americans—Mrs. Herbert Hoover," *Ladies Home Journal,* September, 1917.

MAGAZINE STAFF WRITTEN ARTICES

Good Housekeeping. "The Other Presidents," February, 1932. A well known woman politician sizes up the last five mistresses of the White House.

Iowa Business Woman. "Do You Know Mrs. Hoover of Iowa?" October 1, 1928.

Key of Kappa Kappa Gamma, The. "The Lady of the White House," 1929.

League of Republican Women Magazine, The. "Mrs. Herbert Hoover's Work with Young People," Washington, D.C., November, 1932.

Literary Digest. "Hoover's Silent Partner," September 8, 1917.

———. "Personal Glimpses, Mrs. Hoover's International Housekeeping," November 24, 1928.

Wilcox, Uthai Vincent. "From Machine Guns to First Lady," *Our Young People,* August 10, 1929.

Stanford Alumni Review. "Glimpses of Lou Henry Hoover," 1928.

Western Woman. Hoover Edition of Western Woman, Vol. VII, #9, October, 1932.

Yeoman Shield. "Lou Henry Hoover, the First Lady of the Land," 1929.

Youth's Companion. "Mr. Hoover's Partner," January 17, 1918.

NEWSPAPERS

Burgess, R. L. "Highlights in the Life of Mrs. Hoover," *San Francisco Chronicle,* January 8, 1944.

Clement, Hyde. "Mrs. Herbert Hoover," *New York Herald Tribune,* June 10, 1928.

Comstock, Sara. "A Woman of the West Knocks at the White House Door," *New York Evening Post,* June 16, 1928.

Dougerty, Mary. "Mrs. Hoover's Charm and Grace Win Friends," *New York Evening Journal,* June 15, 1928.

Frazier, Corinne Reid. "Woman's Part in this Era of Readjustment as Carried Out by Mrs. Herbert Hoover," *Sunday Star,* Washington, D. C., January 24, 1932.

Hager, Alice Rogers. "Candidates for Post of First Lady," *New York Times Magazine,* October 2, 1932.

Hoes, Laurence Gouverneur. "Mrs. Hoover's Gift to History," *New York Herald Tribune,* November 6, 1932.

Irwin, Will. "Restoring the Lincoln Study," *Sunday Star,* Washington, D. C., February 9, 1930.

————. "Mrs. Hoover—Pen Portrait by Dare McMullin," As told to Will Irwin, *New York Herald Tribune,* October, 1932.

Mabie, Janet. "Lunch at 1:15 with Mr. and Mrs. Hoover," *Christian Herald,* February, 1932.

McMullin, Dare. See Will Irwin, above.

Peak, Mayme Ober. "Mrs. Hoover as Her California Neighbors Knew Her," *Kansas City Star,* June 24, 1928.

Shepardson, Lucia. "First Lady of the Outdoors," *New York Herald Tribune,* Washington, D. C., March 3, 1929.

Smaus, Jewel Spangler. "The Hoovers of Iowa," *Christian Science Monitor,* April 9, 1960.

Spangler, Jewel. "A Sub Deb Interviewer Gets Interviewed Herself," *Christian Science Monitor,* November 25, 1936.

Wilcox, Uthai Vincent. "Battlefield or Drawing Room," *Brooklyn Eagle,* May 6, 1928.

————. "The Lou Henry Hoover Who Was to Be Our First Lady," *Christian Herald*, June 15, 1929.

Willebrandt, Mabel Walker. "The Religion of Mrs. Herbert Hoover," *Christian Herald*, October 6, 1928.

Witt, Bonita. "Mrs. Herbert Hoover a Charming Hostess," Staff writer for *Central Press Assn.*, Cleveland, 1928.

STAFF WRITTEN ARTICLES

New York Times Magazine. "The Lady of the White House," March 10, 1929.

Society News, Waterloo. "Lou Henry Hoover," March 4, 1921.

Times Herald. "Mrs. Hoover was a Retiring Gracious Lady," Washington, D. C., January 8, 1944.

Washington Post. "Mrs Hoover Seen as Cosmopolitan, Social Worker, Devoted Mother and Real Companion to Husband," November 7, 1928.

Assorted Newspaper clippings from Mrs. Hoover's clipping service.

MISCELLANEOUS MANUSCRIPTS AND PAMPHLETS

Bassett, Emma Naumann. "Lou Henry Hoover School Girl," Manuscript.

Caldwell, Mrs. W. W. "The Hoover Household," in Republican National Committee pamphlet, 1927.

Delkin, James Ladd. "Monterey Peninsula," published by State Department of Education, Berkeley.

Erwin, John. "The History of Academic Costume in America." Intercollegiate Bureau of Academic Costume, 1928.

Large, Jean Henry. Diary.

LaZarre, Eleanor Marie. "Our President's Wife, Lou Henry Hoover," pamphlet, 1931.

Pepper, Elizabeth Neville. "Lou Henry Hoover—The Schoolgirl," for *The Elephant*, a campaign publication, April, 1928.

Rhein, Rev. Victor. "Story of the Paderewski Concert at Stanford sponsored by Mr. Hoover in Student Days," manuscript. South Norwalk, Connecticut.

Wilcox, Uthai Vincent. "Mrs. Hoover as a Home-Maker," *The Republican Woman*, January, 1930.

Witcafski, Christine Vest. "Mountain School, 1930–33," Arlington, Va. Story of the school near Rapidan Camp.

INDEX

263

HELEN BRENTON PRYOR, M.D.

whose mother was a doctor, decided to follow the same profession. After receiving her M.D. degree from the University of Minnesota, she spent five years in China, one at Rockefeller Foundation Hospital, Peking, and four at Nanking University Hospital. Her husband, Roy Pryor, was head of a Middle School for boys. Interrupted by Communist invasion, they escaped on a British gunboat to Shanghai.

Home in California, Roy became Dean of the Menlo School, Helen was appointed to the medical staff at University of California and her mother cared for the two Pryor children.

For ten years, Dr. Pryor was Director of the Women Students Health Service at Stanford University, where she did research and taught Child Growth and Development. She worked closely with Lou Henry Hoover in planning pioneer health activities and related careers for the young women under her care. Later, she resigned to do private pratice.

A Fellow of the American Academy of Pediatrics, she served as Chief of the Pediatrics Staff at Sequoia Hospital and as President of the County Heart Association.

Health and welfare agencies and writing are Dr. Pryor's hobbies. She was President of the Board of Directors of the YWCA, the Volunteer Bureau and Palo Alto's Sister City organization, and served as board member on the County Welfare Council.

She has received medallions for Distinguished Achievement and Distinguished Service from the American Heart Association and Honorary Life Membership in the National Parent-Teacher Association.

Helen B. Pryor, M.D., is author of *As the Child Grows* and co-author of six books in the *American Health Series*. She has published fifty articles in medical journals and several in popular magazines.